All Praises to Mandi's Miracle

"The Miracle Trilogy, by Emeka Iwenofu should be a set of books in every library, in the hands of young adults, and given to those who desire to learn about the law of attraction. This series is sweet and beautifully laid out for those who may have had a tough beginning and feel for certain there must be more to life and it must be good."

—*Debbi Dachinger,*
Syndicated, Award-Winning Host of Dare to Dream Radio,
Bestselling author of Dare to Dream: This Life Counts!

"When I started reading Mandi's Miracle, I thought it was going to be a tragic story about death and grieving. So it was nice when I got to the part where Francine was telling Mandi what to do to get rid of her cancer; it was even more wonderful when it worked. This novel gives hope to readers that no matter what obstacles we encounter, the law of attraction will help us get through it. It is also good to know that whatever disappointments I have, I can just think that maybe it is not meant to be. The story flowed really well, and the incorporation of Francine's lessons was just right. It wasn't like a lecture at all. Emeka Iwenofu wrote this novel in a way that was easy to understand and relate to."

—*Lorena Sanqui*
Readers' Favorite

"Mandi's Miracle *is nothing short of a miracle. It contains all the elements of a great novel. It is funny, down-home, touching, warm, captivating and educational. Emeka masterfully combines a truly creative story with pearls of sage wisdom that the enlightened will cherish. Do yourself a huge favor, read Mandi's Miracle—apply the principles and watch the miracles appear in your life. A dynamic must read!"*

—Josetta Shropshire
Host of the Golden Hope Radio Show
Produced by: Positive Promotions, Ltd. Television & Video Productions

"Mandi's Miracle *is a well-thought-out and highly organized story. The author creates the setting by highlighting major events as well as the unspeakable struggles black people encountered in Mississippi in the 1960's. This gives readers a glimpse of what Mandi and her family had to deal with on top of her life threatening illness. The story also instills the importance of living life with a positive attitude as well as keeping prayer in your heart. Emeka Iwenofu has a gift for storytelling and his ability shines through in this wonderful story that will capture your heart."*

—Stacie Theis
Author, Interviewer, Blogger
and Founder of BeachBoundBooks.com

"Mandi's Miracle *takes an honest soulful look at the life of a Black American family. Full of history and rich with emotional heart tugs. A must read for all seeking the understanding of life."*

—Monique Chapman
Intuitive Consultant, Host of Masterful Choices Radio Show

MANDI'S MIRACLE

Emeka Iwenofu

HOPE POINT PRESS

CLEVELAND

Hope Point Press
PO Box 110452
Cleveland, OH 44111

Cover design by Nate Myers of Wilhelm Design

Subjects of the front cover: Amber Harris, Michelle "Mama Kimba" Posey, & Beverly Weaver

Editors: Connie Garofoli
          Brandy Stuttler

Library of Congress Cataloging-in-Publication Data;

ISBN: 978-0-9855321-8-5
LCCN: 2014910335

mandismiracle.com
Iwenofu, Emeka, Author
Mandi's Miracle / Emeka Iwenofu

.

ePDF ISBN: 978-0-9855321-4-7
ePUB ISBN: 978-0-9855321-7-8

1.   New Thought 2. Health & Wellness 3. Spirituality 4. Law of Attraction.
     Iwenofu, Emeka, Author—A Family Affair

Second Edition

10 9 8 7 6 5 4 3 2 1

This is to those who have battled or are currently battling any health conditions. May this book serve as a guide to what your mind can create once you know its power and act accordingly! Take care.

"*The ultimate measure of a man is not where he stands in moments of comfort and convenience, but where he stands at times of challenge and controversy.*"

—Dr. Martin Luther King Jr.

Contents

Preface..ix

1. A Family Affair 1
2. A Smear of Blood..13
3. The Dreaded Six-Letter Word............................19
4. Awakening...29
5. Mandi's Miracle...48
6. Adolescence...66
7. Midwest Swing...81
8. A Sticky Situation 90
9. Phone Call 101
10. Mrs. Harris 114
11. Pinky Swear 122
12. Something Priceless 136
13. Francine 149
14. Finding Fletch 161
15. New Journey.. 167

Acknowledgments.. 176

Sources... 181

Preface

IF I WERE TO THINK BACK TO WHEN I FIRST FELL IN LOVE with the pen, it would have to be when I was 12 years old and given a writing assignment by my seventh grade teacher, Mrs. Benson, who later said that she enjoyed my story. But if I were to look back to what rooted my talent, I would have to go back to the summer between my fourth and fifth-grade school years with my dad. In order for me to make myself "useful" throughout the summer, rather than watching TV all the time, he'd drop me off with a snack bag at the library before he went to work at 8 a.m. and told me to stay there until he returned from work at 4:30. So in essence, I would be at the library for nearly 8 hours as a means to make myself useful, which for me was to read.

Well, I was not into reading at first. In fact, I hated it, which was why I looked forward to the summer. But with what my father was suddenly implementing for the summer, made me hate it immensely. In fact, I felt my father was being way too harsh on me; almost like he hated me, that I became anxious in knowing if there was some help line service out there that I could report to since I thought this whole act was illegal and a form of child abuse.

Within the first couple days at the library, I grew frustrated and restless, and began annoying the librarians, since I could never stay still at one place. But since it was clear that this was going to be my summer, I eventually picked up "something" to make the best of it. I first started with comic books before actually finding books that seemed interesting. Within a short time, I began bringing books home, suddenly enjoying them, from which my imagination began to take a life of its own, which compelled me to write little short stories by myself, which I enjoyed a lot. As time went on past the seventh grade, I began to get very serious about writing, to where I attended free writers' workshops and wrote two novels on my own by the age of 15 which didn't go anywhere, but convinced me enough that writing was my calling and that I could become a great writer if I was really serious.

As time passed, I decided on getting a major in literature and English from college, which my father later objected to, claiming that I would starve to death. So, as a result, in order to make both my parents "happy", I enrolled at Cleveland State University and took on a much more "sensible" major, which was accounting, since I had somewhat of a gift with crunching numbers in my head. For a while, everything went well and I was due to graduate in a few months, until my life took a whole different direction, one that would alter my path forever.

I was suddenly fired from a federal government position and later with the city government. At that point, I began working a number of odd jobs that were short lived since I had trouble keeping the previous one. At the same time, I was struggling in business ventures of my own, hoping to become a successful entrepreneur based on what was continuing to happen to me in the job market. It was during this time that I began to engage and observe the street life and victims of broken homes, abuse, crime and dysfunctional families. I took mental notes of what I was seeing, learning about their stories, which were totally different from the world I came from that was for the most part, a stable and "normal" setting.

At this time, I began to hate my situation by not being able to provide for myself and having to endure all these massive setbacks without any reasonable breakthrough in sight, and no real explanation of why this was happening. From that point on, I was literally depressed, in despair, and very negative, blaming the system, government, and other institutions for my problems since this was a route I had never anticipated I would ever be in since leaving college. During this time, in order to survive, I became an avid shoplifter (which I felt I was very good at by the way). I also went to abandoned houses, took aluminum and copper, and sold them as scrap metal, while also selling unlawful items to survive. I spent a brief time in corrections for my acts, where I felt I was nothing more than a bitter disappointment to myself and my family; a man wandering about aimlessly without any clear answers or direction in life.

I must say however that it was a pure blessing that I never resorted to alcohol or any other self destructive behavior during this crisis, because I was literally lost.

But as fate would have it, on the day of my birthday, I got a letter in the mail offering me to listen to a CD set on how to obtain success in my life and live the life I always wanted. The cost of the set was $300. At that moment, all I had was $75 along with my car that had no engine in it, which I was going to scrap anyway to get the $300. It was all the money I had to my name that I was now going to use to pay for the course, on strict faith, since I was desperate for a miracle and prayed that this would be the solution to all my problems.

The set ended up becoming the most important invest-ment I had ever made in my life. My whole outlook on life changed, and as a result I read over 20 different books on success and positive principles instructed by the set, which eventually engineered the idea of me writing my first novel as an adult called *Jackie's Miracle*, to share to the world the lessons on how anyone can achieve success throughout all bitter circumstances. This was the start of The Miracle Trilo-gy® series that I published through my company, Hope Point Press.

Francine's Miracle is the first part of the series. The story is of a young Irish immigrant named Francine who immigrates to America during the 1920s. Her family consists of a drunk father, a bitter mother, tragedy, poverty and verbal abuse. She desperately seeks an escape from her problems, so as to enter a better life. It is when she meets a stranger through a twist of fate—who educates her on how to achieve her dreams which forms as a blue print for any reader to do the same in their own lives. It is after Francine applies these techniques and gets her "miracle" that she eventually becomes a mentor in the second book, *Mandi's Miracle*, which takes place during the civil rights movement in 1960s Mississippi.

Mandi is cancer-ridden at a very young age, and receives her "miracle" from mentor Francine, before becoming a pa-role officer and mentor to ex-con, Jackie. *Jackie's Miracle* takes place in the present day, and tells the story of a young woman who lifts herself up from a life of the streets, abuse, drugs, crime, and addiction to personal and professional happiness and prosperity.

I have received tremendous praises by numerous read-ers throughout the world from reading these books already, through my internet blogs or just on the street and hope that they will continue to have a massive and everlasting impact on many more people to come. In just under two years, *Jack-ie's Miracle* has been translated into Japanese with *Francine's*

Miracle next on the way. And because of its impact, I know that there's more translations expected in the near future; all because I just made the decision to write!

But if I were to look back on my life, as to what led me to this point, I would say that everything I have experienced was well worth the price I paid in order to share the idea and knowledge that hope and change are attainable which is why I am so gracious of my past and wouldn't change a thing, since I now know that it was all part of the journey that led me to what I was meant to do in the first place, which is write, and most importantly, share these lessons that can help change a society and impact a culture that so desperately needs it, since that now has become my personal mission and passion in life.

In all, God bless you all, enjoy, and I hope this book helps you realize what's possible, in order to help you achieve your goals and dreams!

—Emeka Iwenofu

PS: Thank you dad for helping me find my talent. You truly knew what you were doing all along and I love you!

1

A Family Affair

MANDI STOOD CROUCHED DOWN ON THE GRASS OF HER backyard, closely watching a beautiful butterfly whirl in front of her before landing at the edge of a lily. The butterfly stood still, not flashing its wings, just a couple of feet from Mandi, who gradually began inching closer to it, trying her hardest not to scare it away. As Mandi approached, the butterfly then began flapping its wings as if it had sensed danger. Yet it still hovered over the lily.

"Gotch ya!" Mandi screamed as she dived upon the lily with both hands clasped together.

But when she opened her hands, all she got was the crumpled lily in her palms, that were scratched from the soil. She then looked up and in front of her was that same butterfly, flying off again. Mandi was so disappointed. This time, she thought she had finally caught herself a butterfly.

"Mandi, get back in the house!" Thelma shouted. "Yo' food's gettin' cold!"

Mandi turned and glanced at the house from which Thelma yelled. "Coming mama," she replied.

Just then, Mandi got up from the grass and went toward the house. As she came in, her mother looked at her. "Dinner's ready. I've been calling you fo' the longest..."

"Sorry," Mandi replied.

"And wash yo' hands. Wipe yo' face. You got grass everywhere, even on your hair," Thelma added while picking some of the grass from Mandi's hair. "You got dirt on yo' pants too, at yo' knees. Lordy lordy, have mercy. I've never seen a girl that loves to play in the dirt as much as you."

"That's because she keeps trying to catch that butterfly. By the way, you caught it yet?" teased her brother Darin, who was suddenly passing through the kitchen with an empty plate from dinner.

Mandi then made a fist trying to attack him. Darin then started laughing, rushing off, but the mother held Mandi, directing her back to the sink to wash her hands.

"You know you'll never catch it," he teased.

"Shut up," Mandi said, before filling a glass of water to throw at him.

Instantly, Darin ducked from the splash, hiding behind the other edge of the wall.

"Missed. You see, you can't catch me. You can't catch anything. What makes you think you can catch a butter... "

"Boy, if you don't hush up and leave her alone, I'll show you a lot of what *I* can catch," her mother retorted as she began hitting Darin against the shoulder as a sign for him to disappear, which he did.

After Mandi was done washing her hands, her mother then took her to the table where her food awaited. On the plate were grits, collard greens, and a drumstick. Immediately Mandi smiled. She loved chicken, but since her family was so large, rarely was there enough to serve everybody. And when there was, one of her siblings always managed to steal whatever was intended for her. But this time her mother secured a drumstick strictly for her.

"Aw, thanks mama," Mandi smiled.

"You're welcome darlin'. But you gone eat all ya food, ya hear? I want'ch ya eatin' dem grits as well as yo greens... *then* the chicken. Miss Francine had a big party today and gave me a buncha meat and leftovers from it... enough to last the family a full week. So jus' eat up."

Mandi then sat in her chair. Soon, her father came from behind, approaching Thelma.

"Thanks beautiful. That food was *good!* Lord have mercy," her father said, kissing her mother on the cheek.

Mandi's mother smiled. "Ya welcome honey."

Mandi's father, Charlie, then put his right hand above her mother's belly gently rubbing it. "You mind if we go upstairs and I show you how grateful I really am? Let me help take the load off. You know I'm good for it. C'mon, let the *docta* take care of you."

Mandi's mother then slapped Charlie's hand. "Now you stop it," she giggled. "We got enough kids as it is, and I'm through havin' anymo."

"Well how 'bout one mo' fo' the road."

"That's what you said before Mandi was born. Then Rosaline was born. And she's now seven."

"Well... you know... things happen." Charlie then began kissing her on the cheek and neck. Mandi, who was struggling with eating her greens, began giggling at the table, hearing everything.

"Go-on, go. Not now," Thelma told him.

Charlie then whispered in her ear, which had Thelma feeling a bit excited. She looked around the back, watching a few of her boys playing football while the others still stood outside chatting with friends who came over to visit. It seemed like Mandi was the only one in the house.

Eventually Thelma staggered away with Charlie.

"Mandi dear, you make sure you eat all yo food now and wash your plates, ya hear? After that, get outta them clothes and take a bath."

"Yes'em," Mandi smirked.

Even though she was only 10, Mandi was no stranger to what was going on. To her, it was enjoyable to know that her father still had the hots for her mother. While other men would beat their wives and run off with other women, her father remained loyal. Her father loved her mother and the whole family. Charlie loved all his children—all 11 of them to be exact. Mandi was the second youngest.

The Watkins family consisted of six boys and five girls. Seven remained at home while the rest lived away. Three were already raising families of their own while one son, Michael, was in the military, serving overseas in Vietnam.

It was the year 1966. Rural Mississippi, where the family lived, had endured almost every racial act of violence imaginable. Segregation was supreme in the South, especially in Mississippi. At an early age, blacks knew certain places were unsafe for them. Signs such as *Whites Only* or *Colored Only* hung over the doorways of movie theatres, hotels, restaurants, bathrooms—even on drinking fountains. And if one was unclear as to where he was unwelcome, someone would let him know... *quick!*

In certain parts of the community, the lynching of black people by whites was hardly anything new. It was a practice that had gone on for decades. There were numerous reports of such cases, which the people of Mississippi heard over and over again, but were rarely investigated. And if the crime *was* properly investigated, the suspects were often acquitted anyway by an all-white jury, similar to the cases of murdered civil rights activist and NAACP leader, Medgar Evers, and 14-year-old, Emmett Till, who was nearly decapitated for allegedly whistling to a white woman.

Emmett, who was originally from Chicago, came to Mississippi to visit family and friends, unaware that the "rules" and ways of people in the South were different from those in the Midwest.

Several days after the whistling incident, according to reports, Emmett was taken from his great uncle's house by a group of angry white men and transported to a barn. While there, he was savagely beaten. One of his eyes was removed and he was shot through the head before being thrown down the Tallahatchie River. His body was found three days later, submerged, as a 70-pound cotton gin had been attached to the barbed wire tied around his neck.

When discovered, Emmett's face was so badly disfigured that he was unrecognizable. If it weren't for the special ring that he wore on his finger, his mother most likely would not have been able to identify him. He had extensive cranial damage, a broken femur, and two broken wrists, which sparked a massive outcry nationally for human equality. Almost no other gruesome act of violence against another human being stood more prevalent than that one did. It was a case that would be remembered for ages to come.

Emmett's mother, Mamie Till-Mobley, authorized for her only child to have an open-casket funeral in order to display the horror and social injustice of blacks in the South. Tens of thousands of people gathered in attendance that day. How the mother lived to be in her 80s, having endured that gruesome act, will forever remain a mystery. She never had any other children after that.

It also wasn't uncommon for blacks to be intimidated not to vote or not attend certain major universities. Even though segregation in schools had been ruled unconstitutional, a number of states were still slow in welcoming integration into certain schools and nationally known colleges.

John F. Kennedy, who was aware of all this as president of the United States, in 1962 fought to allow James Meredith to become the first African-American to attend the University of Mississippi at Oxford, despite the ugly protests and outrage of white citizens, which later led to a huge riot, wounding several people and killing others.

To ensure James's safety, Kennedy ordered a group of soldiers to go to the campus to maintain peace, even though the state's governor at the time was adamantly opposed to Kennedy's decision and furious with the president for giving such a command. But that was the interesting thing about President Kennedy: He made his own decisions and wasn't afraid to use his power. And luckily for James Meredith, he never got hurt and the trouble around him gradually ceased.

Kennedy also ordered the National Guard to help secure African-American students at the University of Alabama, and spoke out that same evening in front of a televised audience, affirming his unwavering support for civil rights and justice for all. In one of his speeches, he stated:

"One hundred years have passed since Abraham Lincoln freed the slaves, yet their heirs, their grandsons, are not fully free. This nation was founded by men of many nations and backgrounds... on the principle that men are created equal."

Kennedy also made this statement, addressing the press, saying:

"...I am asking your help in the tremendous task of informing and alerting the American people, confident that with your help, man will be what he was born to be: free and independent."

Yet during this transition, many blacks would still get objects thrown at them as they went to the voting polls or attended certain college campuses. The Klu Klux Klan would terrorize and harass blacks during the night, ensuring that they stayed away from white communities and ceased to engage in any demonstrations against inequality. Blacks were prohibited from going to certain schools, grocery stores and other businesses for no other reason except for the simple fact that they were one thing: colored.

Yet ironically, life wasn't easy for some whites either. There were a number of cases of whites who led in the fight for racial equality before eventually paying for it with their own lives. So while some whites had compassion for other races, if they dared express it in an open demonstration, they soon became instant targets by angry whites.

Such white martyrs included Reverend James Reeb, Viola Gregg Liuzzo, and the two young Jewish men, Andrew Goodman and Michael Henry Schwerner, who, along with their black friend, James Earl Chaney, were shot and killed before their bodies were buried in an earthen dam by local Mississippi Klansmen. All three men were no older than 24. In all, hatred was deeply imbedded in the South. Deeply.

However, there were peaceful protests, restaurant sit-ins, and different boycotts organized as a means for change. Many were led by none other than the Honorable Reverend Dr. Martin Luther King Jr.. Dr. King, who was friends with President Kennedy, was promoting justice and peace throughout North America through non-violent means, a principle he had studied and learned extensively from Mahatma Gandhi of India, who used such methods to overthrow the British Empire.

In one of his speeches, Dr. King said, *"Injustice anywhere is a threat to justice everywhere."* What a powerful quote. In other words, no one is free while others are oppressed.

The Watkins family was fully aware of the racial tensions that existed throughout their community, which was why they never participated in anything that would spur any 'trouble' against them. Ignoring what went on and going about their business was how they knew to survive. Any acts of revolution committed by them of any sort could result in mere suicide. All they wanted was to be left alone so they could come home safely. At least that's what the parents, Charlie and Thelma, tried to instill in all of their children.

There were of course the occasional social altercations which most of the children experienced to some degree with other white people. However, there were none too serious to cause any major harm to the family, which everyone was grateful for.

Charlie was a hardworking man. He was a blacksmith, always banging steel in the factory he worked in. The wages were never as much as he wanted. Yet it was still a job and he liked doing it. What he loved most were the people he would meet and talk to. Nothing made him happier than to chat with people and put a smile on their faces after they did business. Blacksmithing was all he had ever done, having learned the trade as a teenager, before meeting his wife Thelma.

He hadn't much education. He could barely read or write. His parents never enrolled him in any school, which left him with no other duties but physical labor, such as cooking, cleaning around the house, going to the store, or running errands. At 14, a good friend of his father's introduced him to blacksmithing, and he began to work as much as he could to bring money home for the family.

Charlie was from a big family as well. He had three brothers and four sisters. He was the fifth oldest child. So as he got older, his other siblings began working, which eventually allowed him to venture off to have his own place to live. His main hobby was going out with the boys, drinking every once in a while. He also just loved to dance, and caught the eye of Thelma one night at a local jazz club.

There were different entertainers playing all the time at the club, where music from the drums, piano, trumpets and harmonica reigned supreme, and the dance floor was especially large. It took on the name *Southern Swang*, while others called it *soul*. After Charlie stopped dancing momentarily, the lovely Miss Thelma just looked at him while moving her head to the beat, later catching his attention. So without hesitation, Charlie went over to her as she smiled, standing right next to her girlfriends.

"Hello lady, how do you do?" he greeted her, taking off his hat.

"Fine, yo'self?"

"I'm doin' mighty fine now that *you're* here."

"Wow. I nevuh heard that before. Tell me something, do you say this to *all* the ladies you see fo' the first time?"

Charlie then looked down, before raising his head again. "Uh... no," he said. "I'm afraid you're the first... and hopefully... the last."

Thelma shook her head in excitement.

Charlie, not really knowing what to make of it, asked a question. "You don't mind if I talk to you, do you?"

Thelma looked at him emphatically. "I don't know. *Can* you?" she replied.

The two both laughed. Then, about a minute later, Charlie cleared his throat, trying not to laugh as he answered, "I sho' can."

"Well all right," she smiled.

Charlie thought while seeing Thelma wait in anticipation. "Okaaay... tell me, what's yo' name darlin'?" he asked.

"Thelma."

"Oh... Thelma. Is that right?"

"Yes suh. Thelma Washington. How 'bout yuhself?"

"Oh... well they call me, Charlie. Charlie Watkins," he smiled. "Say Thelma, you wanna dance?"

"Me?"

"Well, I'own know any othuh Thelma 'round here. Do you?"

Thelma instantly turned around, looking at her girl-friends before facing Charlie. "Well... I... I can't. I can't... da... da... *dance*," she said.

"Wait, you mean to tell me that you's a black woman and you can't dance?" Charlie asked.

Thelma nodded slowly.

"Well in that case, I'll be yo' instructor fuh this evening. C'mon."

"But... but... "

"Ain't no buts now. Just follow my lead."

Just then, Charlie yanked Thelma off to the dance floor where she began to feel a bit embarrassed, thinking there was nothing left to do but to watch Charlie and follow his routine. Within minutes, she began enjoying herself and stayed with him for quite a while, later getting the hang of the routine. He had all the good moves on the dance floor, which seemed quite impressive, judging from the suspenders he wore across his shirt, which didn't appear to limit him one bit.

The two of them began swinging both their feet together before turning around in rhythm, moving their hips. Charlie would then flip her in the air before catching her as she land-ed—a routine that was most common among all the danc-ers. Both of them were in pure sweat by the time they were finished

Shortly after, their eyes met and Charlie kissed her on the lips, which had Thelma blushing, feeling quite shy. From that point on, they both knew that things would nev-er be the same again. They would see more of each other constantly as time went on. A year passed and they were married. Thelma was already pregnant a few months pri-or. However, Charlie had already chosen her as his mate. She would be his and his alone, even though they were still teenagers at the time.

Thelma was quite similar to Charlie. She too came from a large family and had limited schooling. She wasn't good at writing and could only read to a certain extent, which was only because she needed to in order to prepare food from the special recipes her mother gave to her. Her mother, who was a maid for white people, later showed her the trade from which Thelma took on shortly before she met Charlie.

Since they were both working, they were able to secure a home of their own. That same year they had a son, named Charlie Jr.. Then, after him, came Tammy, then Martha, followed by Michael, Jimmy, Kyle, Carla, Calvin, Darin, Mandi, and Rosaline—just the typical family size.

But Thelma was very clear about not having any more children. She didn't want any more of the discomfort that came with it. And besides, she already outdid her mother, who had seven. So what more did she have to prove? And at 44, she was through. The pleasure was still fun, yet she just didn't want to have to pay for it anymore. According to her, she had paid enough.

Soon after, Mandi was done with her meal. It soon got dark and the rest of the siblings later gathered in the house from which the commotion never ceased.

"Mandi, where's mama and papa?" asked Calvin.

"In their room, but I suggest you don't go there. They're… they're… you know… " she tried gesturing.

"I know 'what'?"

"Shackin' up," she giggled.

Calvin then began chuckling as well. The term "shackin' up" usually referred to making love. "Girl, what you know 'bout that anyway?" he asked.

"Nothin'. I jus' knew that was what they was gone do."

"Well, if care ain't taken, mama and papa go'n mess around and have enough fo' a football team with me as the quarterback."

Together, they both laughed.

"But I thought mama was through havin' kids," Calvin whispered.

Mandi shrugged her shoulders. "I guess… it's like money. It just ain't nevuh enough."

Calvin laughed. To him, Mandi was too smart for her age. After a few minutes, she proceeded to the kitchen, attempting to scrape off the rest of the grits and greens in the dumpster.

"Aw, I'm tellin'. I know mama told you to eat dem grits and greens," stated Rosaline, who just happened to appear in the kitchen. She was the youngest.

"So! Mama won't believe you and you bet' not go in that room anyway. She's… she's busy with papa."

"Doing what?" Rosaline wondered.

"Ya… you'll understand later. Now go on now," demanded Mandi.

Rosaline paused for a moment. "Well, I'm still tellin'," she said, stomping away.

After Rosaline disappeared, the rest of the family began sprinkling everywhere within the house before eventually going to bed with Jimmy as the leader, who ensured such was the case. He was the oldest sibling left living in the house. Therefore, the parents always entrusted him to carry out the orders when they weren't around or "busy."

Mandi however, did change her clothes and took a bath, which she needed as a result of the itchy feeling she kept on getting from laying on the grass. When she changed into cleaner clothes, she stayed at the edge of the bed facing the wall as three other siblings later pressed against her for room they needed for sleep. Within an hour, everyone was asleep, which signaled peace and quiet momentarily in the Watkins' home.

2

A Smear of
Blood

SKEEGEE, MISSISSIPPI, WHERE THE WATKINS FAMILY
lived, was a predominantly black rural town, located just
20 miles south of Jackson. The community mostly consisted
of black businesses and working class Americans. A good
percentage of the people owned restaurants, corner stores,
barber shops, shoe shine parlors and mechanic shops. Most
residents of the town did business with other blacks, thereby
putting money back into the community.

The community was tight-knit as well. Virtually everyone
knew everyone else's business and looked out for each other.
So for example, if a young child was caught misbehaving, a
stranger would come from nowhere and spank the child, demanding to see his or her parents. Once that child directed
the stranger to the parents, one of the parents, usually the
mother, would be informed of the situation and would later
spank that child again for having to be reprimanded by a
stranger, and the stranger and the mother would eventually

become good friends. That's just how it was. The motto was, that since the government and law enforcement didn't look out for them, they had to look out for each other.

Gossip ran deep in the community as well. Certain people who knew other people's business would spread it throughout the area, often giving their own versions of what really happened. Therefore it was important not to ever do anything embarrassing in the public eye, because the news was definitely sure to get out.

The town had been both Charlie's and Thelma's home since their childhood days. Both their grandparents had been slaves from Mississippi and would tell their grandchildren stories of their experiences, which they would hear time and time again.

What most people didn't know, however, was that Mandi's name was actually spelled by accident. Her parents, who were for the most part illiterate, weren't all that good at spelling. Their other children, who were all slightly more proficient in spelling, were also present during Mandi's birth. However, they were so involved with the new life in front of them that no one really bothered to care how her name was being spelled. Therefore when Mandi was born, the parents immediately assumed that the normal spelling of her name carried an 'i' at the end instead of a 'y,' which was exactly what they wrote on her birth records. However, it wasn't until a few of the other children later discovered Mandi's name on an official document mailed to them that the parents suddenly realized their "mistake." They really weren't planning on being *unique* at all. Rather, they would have preferred the traditional spelling, just like it should have been.

But it was partly this that caused the parents to believe that education was so important. They believed it was power. And it was their dream to see that all of their children went to school, and hopefully off to college. Although, they saw it best to leave the decision up to the children instead of forcing it down their throats, since after all, they never went to school.

Thelma and Charlie, however, did try their best to set good values for their children. Each child was taught early on their role in the household, and did so accordingly. Therefore laziness was never an option. It just wasn't. Both parents emphasized hard work and that regardless of any circumstance, family was to always stick together, no matter what.

However, Thelma had no problem spanking her kids. She believed wholeheartedly in using the rod rather than sparing it. To her, that was the best method she knew of to get her point across. Charlie was more lenient towards the idea, especially when it came to the boys. But not Thelma. No. She was at times so lethal with her belt that sometimes the children were afraid to come home. And Mandi was no exception. They all got the switch.

A couple years would go by and one day Mandi, along with her mother and a few siblings, went to the grocery store to get some food for the house. Mandi, who trailed behind on her way to the store, was not feeling well. She was feeling a little light-headed and dizzy. When her mother turned around to see what was wrong, Mandi just stood still for a moment as if she wanted to vomit or urinate.

"Mandi, would you just come on and quit playin' around?" reacted Thelma. "This is not the time. C'mon now."

Mandi looked at her. "But… I'm not… playin' mama. Somethin'… somethin's wrong," she said, softly.

"What is it dear?" Thelma asked, coming closely.

Suddenly, Mandi dropped to the ground on her knees, which soon had her mother and everyone else in a panic. They then immediately rushed over to see what was wrong.

"Baby, what's the mattuh? Please tell yo' mama," pleaded Thelma.

Mandi then began holding her nose for almost a minute, unwilling to let go. When Thelma asked her why she wouldn't let go, Mandi wouldn't respond.

"Let go," said Thelma. "Let go."

Soon Thelma began reaching to remove Mandi's hand from under her nose, yet Mandi struggled to keep it on. When she finally did let go, a gush of blood began oozing out of her nose, which eventually touched the ground, smearing Mandi's hand. The blood soon reached her overalls. Thelma was in complete shock, not knowing what to do. The other siblings were in shock as well. However her brother, Calvin, went quickly to get a tissue to place on Mandi's nose to stop the bleeding, which did help a little.

"Get some more," demanded Thelma, holding the tissue.

Calvin did and placed more on Mandi's nose.

At that point, Thelma decided to skip the grocery shopping and take everyone back home. Mandi just held the tissue as her brothers, Calvin and Darin, helped her to the car. The store owner, who saw the stained pavement in front of the store, suddenly demanded who was going to clean the mess up. Yet, the family escaped just in time before the owner could catch them.

When Mandi got home, she was laid down on the bed with a trickle of blood still dripping slightly, which wasn't nearly as much as before. After about 30 minutes, the bleeding stopped and Mandi rested her head down, looking to the ceiling. Eventually one of her sisters, Carla, came to give her some tea, which she drank. Carla and the others became concerned and started asking how it happened.

Mandi had no idea and claimed that it had been the third time that such a thing occurred. However the first two incidents were little droplets. Shortly after, their father came to announce to Mandi that they would be seeing a doctor by the following week. It could have been earlier, but Thelma wasn't due to get paid at her job by Francine until the coming Monday.

When they got to the clinic, both Charlie and Mandi waited in the lobby. The wait took nearly one hour, but they were eventually seen. When Charlie explained to the doctor what had been happening, the doctor proceeded to examine Mandi. At that moment, nothing appeared wrong. There was no blood anywhere and Mandi appeared to be fine. The doctor then instructed that she do some activities with her face pointed downwards, from which she did. There didn't appear to be any blood.

As a result, the doctor then decided that since they couldn't identify a problem as of yet, that some blood work and a body scan be conducted to identify her overall state of health. Charlie agreed and decided that they would be ready in a few weeks for that. By then, he was sure that both he and Thelma would have enough money to afford such tests. The doctor then responded, "will do." After that, he shook Charlie's hand, greeted Mandi, and wished them the best.

However, he did remind Charlie not to delay getting Mandi tested. According to him, there could be a serious condition that no one was aware of, which may need to be detected right away before it got real severe. Charlie took his advice and ensured that he'd be ready to afford the testing in a few weeks.

As soon as Charlie and Mandi walked out, they suddenly saw several people running in the streets with weapons, on the verge of committing some violent acts. Some of them carried either sticks, baseball bats, or homemade flame throwers, which began to land in empty buildings. Soon after, there was loud music everywhere with people jumping on cars, screaming. A few white people, who had nothing to do with this whatsoever, began running away scared from the angry black people who chased after them. It was total mayhem.

Charlie and Mandi had to soon duck for cover, shielding their heads as they proceeded to the bus stop. Some bottles were thrown and store windows were shattered. Neither

Charlie nor Mandi could determine what was going on. All they could think of was that something major had happened that was causing all this menace. Because they were in Mississippi, they were highly aware that certain communities could bring about rage like this, based on the state's history of violence. But to them, these acts were so sudden. So they were anxious to know what had happened. Hopefully, it wasn't another Emmett Till incident.

When they had finally arrived home safely, they immediately shut their doors, fearing that some people were after them. Once back in the house, Charlie immediately laid his back against the door, demanding an explanation.

"Calvin, Carla, Darin, or Jimmy… any one of you. Can someone please tell me just what the hell is goin' on here? There's so much madness out there in the streets that me and Mandi had to duck for cover all the way home. We're lucky we didn't get hurt."

"Haven't you heard?" Jimmy asked, looking a bit surprised.

"Heard what?" Charlie asked.

"Yeah, heard what?" added Mandi, rubbing her nose.

"Dr. Martin Luther King Jr. He was shot… "

"Dead," finished Carla.

"Are you serious? Where?" wondered Charlie.

"On a balcony, somewhere… in Memphis," Carla replied. "It's all on the radio."

"Yeah," added Calvin. "That's why people are out in the streets angry. It's great y'all made it back safe. I'd suggest stayin' home for a few days… if you can, because it's gone get crazy for a while."

Just then, Charlie fell down to a chair, feeling deflated as he began rubbing his forehead, speechless. He appeared like he was in a daze. First Kennedy. Then Malcolm X. Now Martin Luther King Jr. What was this world coming to? Mandi, who also loved Dr. King, suddenly ran to her bed, crying.

3

The Dreaded Six-Letter Word

Two weeks went by and Mandi was admitted back into the clinic. She underwent a blood test and a body scan, and the doctor suggested that the family return back the next week to see the results.

Within that week, however, Mandi began to have massive headaches. She started becoming dizzy, suddenly complaining about being tired and weak. While this was going on, she was in the seventh grade at school, and the illness was causing an increasing number of absences. Soon, all the siblings began to get concerned, checking her temperature as she lay in bed.

When it finally became time to return for the results, Thelma, Charlie and Mandi set out for the clinic. When they arrived in the doctor's office, the doctor seemed a bit uneasy. Thelma then brought a smile to the room. However, the doctor was unresponsive and seemed a bit ill-at-ease, as if it was difficult to do anything else. That alone instantly changed

Thelma's expression as well, fearing that something was definitely wrong.

"How are you all doing?" the doctor asked softly.

"Mighty fine," Thelma smiled. "Everyone's fine."

"Well how's Mandi?"

Thelma paused for a moment. "Well... she'll get bettuh. She's been havin' a lot of headaches lately and has been weak all the time. But she'll pull through. I know she will. She's my baby. There's nothin' that the Watkins can't do."

"*Yes ma'am*," Charlie added in melodic tune.

"So, what you got fo' us doc? Please tell me it's nothin' serious."

"Well... if you want me to say that, I could, *but* it wouldn't be the truth."

Just then, Thelma's mood changed completely along with Charlie, who suddenly sat up straight trying to be all ears. "Well, what's wrong?" he asked.

The doctor stood still for a moment. "Is it possible maybe you can have Mandi wait outside while I tell you... "

"No, no. She's not goin' anywhere," retorted Thelma. "Now this is *her* diagnosis and she aught to know what's happenin' with huh. So go 'head doc, shoot it to us straight. We can take it. I've given birth to eleven chil'ren. So I know I can take anything. So, c'mon wit' it."

The doctor then looked at Mandi who was just as anxious, but fearful at the same time of what she was about to hear. "Okay, fair enough," he said, still in a soft tone. "Your daughter here, Mandi Watkins, has... *cancer*."

Thelma's heart sank. "What? Wait hol' up," she said. "You said she has *what*?"

The doctor cleared his throat. "Cancer," he said.

"That's what I thought you said, now... "

Charlie suddenly interrupted. "But how can this be? I mean... "

"Wait, wait Charlie," insisted Thelma. "You'll get your turn, I promise. I'm talkin' here." She then turned to the doctor. "So doc, tell me. How could this be?"

"It could have happened for a variety of reasons. Just know it was nothing you did or could have done. So it's not your fault or her's either. The screen shows cancer spreading around her midsection and near her chest area. From such symptoms come high fevers, dry mouth, headaches, weakness, stomach problems, chest pains and other ailments."

Suddenly, Thelma began to drop a tear, looking at Mandi in the eyes. That would explain why she was having the problems she was having. The symptoms all went parallel to what the doctor was saying. "So what do we do now, doc? Like... how can we get rid of the cancer?"

"I'm afraid there's no cure for cancer as of yet. So... all I can suggest is to give her some medication that will help control the disease and keep it from spreading."

"So what you're saying is that she's gonna continue havin' these problems *forever...* you mean non-stop?"

The doctor was silent for a moment. "That may be true," he said.

"So you're saying she may live in this agony forever and... *die?*"

"Mrs. Watkins, this by no means is easy for me to explain... "

"Don't you dare patronize me! Understand? Now just tell me! Is she going to die from this disease?"

"Mrs. Watkins, many people have been known to die from... "

"I'm gone tell you one mo' time. Don't you dare Mrs. Watkins me. I'll tell you when I need for you to be fo'mal. Now just tell me. Will my daughter eventually die from this disease?"

"Well, judging from the analysis and fact that there is no cure, as of yet... yes, she will."

At that moment, Thelma had wanted to faint. She was through asking questions. Mandi, who tried to hold her up, was totally distraught and had wished she was in the waiting area never hearing such news. The word 'cancer' is something you don't wish on anyone. It is such an uncomfortable word to talk about. The only time when it's ever convenient is when one uses it to describe a person's zodiac sign.

"I'm really sorry Mr. and Mrs. Watkins," added the doctor. "And I'm sorry for you too, Mandi."

Charlie, not knowing what else to do, went up and shook the doctor's hand, understanding that it wasn't easy for him to report the matter. And from Charlie's point of view, no matter how bitter the truth was, it was better that the family knew rather than not knowing.

"However, I do want to recommend some medications she can take," the doctor said, suddenly shifting to a nearby counter. "What I have with me are three medications. One is Ojentin. The other is Xribal. And the third is Plaxico."

He then went on explaining the uses for each medication and the times Mandi was to take them. He said that they would control the pain and keep the cancer from spreading, which could help prolong her life. At age 12, it was uncertain how long she could live, but with the medications, hopefully she could graduate high school, which is what the doctor intended on. However, the doctor recommended that Mandi report to him periodically so he could see the extent of her condition, and could recommend other options if needed.

After that, the family went home in a state of shock. Mandi's siblings, who saw the mood on her face along with their parents, seemed puzzled and anxious to find out what had happened. When they eventually heard the news, they were in states of panic, fear, and helplessness. Darin, who often teased his sister, wasn't laughing any longer. Everyone was at a loss of words, unable to know what to do. Thelma then showed them the medications, from which Darin volunteered to give them to Mandi as directed.

What was so interesting was that no one in the family ever had any major disease, except for the common flu or chicken pox. So how Mandi developed this disease was beyond anyone's comprehension. From Thelma's family tree, she knew no one who was gravely ill—and neither did Charlie. Yet even if they did, that wasn't important anymore. The fact was Mandi needed everyone's support in helping her get through this battle.

In her heart were conditions of fear and worry. She didn't want to die, and couldn't conceive how any of this could be happening to her. Though, no one felt the condition worse than Thelma. For several nights, she had difficulty sleeping, and she attended to Mandi often to make sure she was okay or to check if she needed anything. Mandi however, was able to walk and move. It's just that she did things a little slower and grimaced a little more whenever she moved certain body parts.

Nearly a year went by and Mandi's condition began to worsen. She had dry mouth and her voice would sometimes sound hoarse. Her skin also appeared rough and suddenly she was unable to walk or stand straight. She often cried over the disease, but sometimes it was just because her body hurt so much. She began to lose weight because she often refused food as a result of the stomach pain.

Her siblings tried their best to comfort her. Carla would read certain stories to her while Darin tried to entertain her with funny jokes. Darin was always a prankster and very funny. Rosaline, the youngest, would bring Mandi flowers she would find in open fields on her way back from school. This all felt good and made Mandi smile a lot. The love from family can never be explained unless one experiences it. She was so happy. The Watkins family could be described in many ways, but love for one another was a characteristic that symbolized the most of what they truly were.

Yet with the pain persisting, she often changed her mood, always grimacing, hoping that it wouldn't be as profound provided that she took her medication—which she did periodically. By this time, her medication had gone from three to seven different bottles. And yet, she still was not getting better.

Such expenses were very distressing to Charlie and Thelma. Nearly half of their wages went towards Mandi's medical needs alone. They were now taking her to see the doctor almost every two weeks, a frequency that was only increasing.

When Charlie and Thelma brought their daughter back this time, a nearly helpless Mandi tiptoed in with her parents and waited for the doctor. There were more test results to go over from the last visit.

When the doctor finally called them in, Mandi insisted that she wait in the lobby while her parents went in to talk with the doctor. Every time she went inside the doctor's office, it became an agonizing experience for her. So this time she wanted to stay in the waiting room. In turn, the doctor agreed with her and suggested he talk to Thelma and Charlie alone. Her parents then left her and proceeded in.

"I'm afraid I have bad news," the doctor said.

"What?" asked Thelma.

"Well, judging from the report, the cancer has developed throughout other parts of her body. It's now affecting her liver. It's in part of her bones, in her chest; almost everywhere. I had hoped that the medications would help control the spread, but I'm afraid they didn't."

"So what do we do now?" Charlie wondered.

The doctor then bowed his head. "I'm afraid there is… nothing you can do at this point. As much as I hate saying this, and trust me I do… "

"Just say it!" demanded Thelma.

"Okay, here goes. Start... making... funeral arrangements."

"What do you mean funeral arrangements?" asked Charlie.

"Mr. Watkins, the cancer has spread virtually everywhere. It's practically hopeless. She's just riddled with cancer. No kind of immune system can combat the disease now. It's in her organs, in her tissue. It's only a matter of time before those functions fail... and they will. I can guarantee it."

"How long?" The doctor then began gesturing with his hands trying his best not to answer the question. "You're the doctor! How long?" Charlie repeated.

"From what the records indicate, my prediction is... four to six months."

"Four to six months? That's it?" replied Thelma softly. "My baby's gonna die in four to six months?"

"I'm truly sorry, Mrs. Watkins."

Thelma was suddenly hysterical. "What do you mean, sorry? But we trusted you. You promised that the medications would work. You promised. Now I'm gonna lose my baby!"

Suddenly she moved forward to try and attack the doctor. Charlie held her back. "Parents are never supposed to bury their kids! Kids are supposed to bury their parents!" she exclaimed in tears, before hugging Charlie. Soon her voice got much louder.

"Okay, calm down, calm down, baby," pleaded Charlie.

"What do you mean calm down? We're going to lose our baby and you're telling me to calm down!"

Suddenly, she fell to the floor, wailing helplessly. "Why God, why? What did I do?" she cried.

This went on for a few more minutes before Charlie eventually picked her up from the floor and guided her to the exit where Mandi awaited them. Mandi was, of course, eager to discover what the problem was. However, it was something neither parent had the courage to say. And no matter how much Mandi begged, they kept it quiet. They chose to not even inform the siblings. However, the tone of Thelma's voice showed more had happened during that the visit than just a usual check-up. Yet both parents decided not to reveal what was discussed until they could discover a solution.

During this time, Thelma became an avid prayer. Yet the worry and fear in her distracted her ability to finish most prayers. Her emotions affected nearly every facet of her life. They affected her job, her communication with her kids, her marriage with Charlie—everything. There was never a day that went by when she didn't worry about Mandi. She was desperate for a miracle, but didn't quite know how to get it. Meanwhile, Mandi's condition grew worse and worse, and she started coughing uncontrollably. And every time her family saw her suffer, it brought pain and tears to their eyes, thinking there was nothing they could do.

Thelma held the job of head maid of her boss's estate. Her employer was Francine Williamson, the owner of the estate. Thelma had worked there for over 25 years. She was the oldest maid working there. The maid who had been there the second longest had only worked there 10 years, therefore Thelma had seniority over everyone there, directing them as their head boss. She had always arrived on time and never once called off, unless it was a maternity leave issue. That was it. Even if she was sick, she still came to work. That was just the kind of woman Thelma was. She was committed to her work and in seeing that everything was to Francine's satisfaction—and Francine respected her for that.

About a month after Mandi's last doctor's visit, a distraught Thelma suddenly dropped a large tray of dishes on the kitchen floor that carried meals for Francine's guests. Francine, who was in the dining room with her guests, heard the clang and instantly went to check what had happened.

When she arrived, she was shocked to see Thelma, who had never cried before, sobbing like a helpless child.

Surprised by the whole thing, Francine immediately went over to find out what was the matter. Thelma then began explaining that her second youngest child was dying of cancer, and that the doctor said that she had approximately 4 to 5 months left to live.

Moved by the comment, Francine tried to encourage Thelma to calm down. However, Thelma went on wailing until her subordinates began entering the kitchen to see what was going on. Francine commanded them to leave the room immediately and get back to work. Yet Thelma continued wailing. Not knowing how to calm her down, Francine suddenly made a powerful statement to Thelma—one that Thelma would never forget.

Francine said: "Now look, Thelma. Either you get yourself together right this minute and listen to what I have to say, or be ready to put a whole bunch of flowers on your daughter's grave, which will happen a lot quicker than when the doctors predict, I assure you. You understand? So you decide right now!"

Upon hearing that, Thelma calmed down. Francine then suggested that she would help her daughter fight the cancer, which will in turn cure her of the disease—if she's willing. But it would have to be her choice.

Thelma then pleaded that Francine do so. Francine in turn, accepted. Though there were a few stipulations. Mandi had to come to Francine's house for a couple of hours three times a week so that she could administer to Mandi the "healing" process.

Secondly, since she was investing time with Mandi, Thelma would have to agree to only receiving half of her normal wages during the process. What that meant was that Thelma would only work part time during that period, since she was going to be accompanying her daughter to these visits. For a moment, Thelma was a bit upset over the thought of the change, but quickly realized that if it was going to save her daughter's life, then no amount of money could ever match what they were about to experience.

Francine had a gentle spirit. She was very sympathetic in moments like this because she could easily relate. She came from humble beginnings, from a poor Irish family who had immigrated to the United States when she was 8 years old. It wasn't until someone exposed her to a secret that her entire life changed for the better. This was now her way of giving back.

The second reason why Francine chose to help Thelma was simply because she liked her very much. Apart from all the staff, Thelma was the one who was most loyal, held a great work ethic, and had committed over a quarter century serving Francine. To Francine, those were priceless qualities one couldn't measure with money. One either had that gift or didn't—and Thelma had it. So to Francine, it was only fair to return the favor. To reward something so priceless, Francine thought, required something equally as priceless, which in her case was knowledge; similar to what she had experienced during her own childhood.

4

⁓⁓⁓

Awakening

Francine Williamson, now in her 50s, was a petite brunette who took good care of herself, and always had since her youth. She kept a slim frame at a height of 5'7 and 140 pounds. Her still youthful glow was accentuated by blue eyes and freckles softly dotting her cheekbones. She tried to maintain a smile wherever she went, exposing her dimples, which made her facial expression all the more appealing to anyone who looked at her. She was the mother of nine children, all of whom were already grown and since moved out, which made her feel a bit lonely at times. Yet, she still had close ties with each one of them and they all would visit her periodically.

Francine had been married for 31 years to a man named John Williamson, who died a few years after having suffered a stroke on his way home from work one day. He was 61 years old. The pursuit of trying to "control" everything became such an obsession with him that he rarely took the time to relax and enjoy life—a trait quite similar to his own father, George Williamson, who also died of a stroke.

John's stroke left him paralyzed from the neck down, which prevented him from working at the office as a banker. He often sat in a wheelchair, whereby Francine and others wheeled him around to wherever he had to go. What was worse was that he was starting to have difficulty remembering things, which had Francine in a state of tears, looking at him struggle to remember the fun times they shared from the pictures she would show him. Her husband, who was always so determined and confident, able to take on any task at hand during the recent years, now laid helpless and weak. It was a very challenging moment in Francine's life.

At times others suggested she take her husband to a nursing home, where she was told he'd get the best care money could buy. But Francine adamantly objected. According to her, John was getting the best care he deserved, which was with her, and over her dead body was anyone going to change that. As far as she was concerned, John made one of the biggest sacrifices one could ever make for someone else, which was marrying her despite everyone else's objections, which made John decide to depart from their presence in order to live the rest of his life with Francine in peace. And it was that act alone that created enough reason for Francine to return the favor. But she knew that taking on such a task would in no way be easy... at all.

Taking care of John required almost around-the-clock care. When he woke up, he had to be carried to a wheelchair to be transported to the bathroom where he bathed, before being dressed to prepare for breakfast where he was spoon-fed his meals or given bits of toast to chew on. Afterwards, he would be wheeled around his garden, observing nature, where he and Francine would engage in some laughter like old times. Because John was her husband, Francine knew exactly what he was trying to say, even if no one else understood.

Eventually, his immobility and lack of office work forced John into a state of depression, making him want to give up on life in general. Francine tried to cheer him up, but John just felt less of a man due to his physical condition and having lost all ties to his former career. And it was because of this internal rage and anger that one beautiful Monday morning he never woke up. It was one of *the* saddest moments in Francine's life.

Though despite everything, Francine vowed never to marry again. She loved John so much that she decided he was to be her last and only soul mate. John was her heart and her dream come true. And no man could *ever* replace that as far as she was concerned. No one.

Every other Saturday, Francine would religiously go to John's grave site to set new flowers there while removing the old ones she had placed two weeks earlier. She would stand beside his grave for a few minutes, touching his tombstone, say a short prayer, then kiss his tombstone before leaving. That was her routine.

As a result of his death, however, Francine was given full control of his estate, which she later distributed as best she could amongst her children as a means of carrying on their father's legacy—which, for the most part, paid off.

A number of the children pursued business ventures and careers that helped secure their livelihoods and beyond; while a couple of them used the money for foolish reasons. *JW Loan & Associates*, which was John's lending service, was eventually taken over by Francine's oldest son, Jacob.

It wasn't a secret; the Williamson family was rich. John was the son of a wealthy land owner, which allowed him the capital needed to build the luxurious home the entire family lived in, along with several businesses that fueled more wealth. So, money was never an issue. In the beautiful mansion she still lived in, Francine employed six maids, two butlers, three cooks, one chauffeur, four gardeners, and two people who tended the horses. Never were their wages ever late, which was always a good feeling.

Francine devoted much of her time to reading. Over the years she read from a collection of books on the development of the mind and body. If she wasn't reading, she'd take rides to famous malls to shop or eat at fancy restaurants. At times she would take walks around open fields to relax her mind or play with her white miniature poodle named *Snowy*, where she threw a Frisbee or tennis ball for her to catch. Francine also liked carrying Snowy around and showing everyone how adorable she was.

If there was still time during the day, Francine would stop by her boutique to check on the flow of business and pick up any cash if needed. She sometimes spent time at home entertaining guests with a game of bridge, chess—or just socializing.

She would take mini vacations from time to time, traveling to places like Paris, London, Sweden, Ireland, and parts of America, either to visit her siblings or just tour the country, learning more and more about the world around her. She loved traveling. Traveling was a necessity in her mind that every man needed. From it she thought, all bigotry and prejudice among people would cease, as a result of the knowledge obtained from travel.

She was very social as well, always establishing personal relationships with her staff members, with a talent for knowing just how to cheer them up. She was also funny at times. And, she was going to do her best to heal Mandi's condition. Although this would be Francine's first assignment working with a person of ill health, she felt more than confident that she would succeed, just provided that her subject followed her instructions as directed.

Francine saw this process as a means for her to finally unleash the principles she learned from the books she read over the years, as well as the teachings she acquired through her mentor, Mary Jo, who she met back in Virginia, before her marriage to John.

When Thelma finally arrived at Francine's multi-acre estate with her daughter, Mandi was immediately astounded by the villa. Her eyes brightened in amazement, marveling at everything that stood before her, and this was just on the outside. There were flowers surrounding the building, and beautifully trimmed bushes that bordered the entire entranceway to the house. The grass was dark green, with not a single weed in sight.

With the help of her mother, Mandi was pushed along in a wheelchair to meet Francine for the first time, who seemed mighty pleased to meet her.

"Good afternoon, Francine dear," Thelma greeted, removing her hat.

"Good afternoon... And you must be Mandi, the young child who has come to see me today?"

Mandi lifted her head. "Yes ma'am. Good afternoon. You have a wonderful place ma'am. I like it very much already."

"Thank you."

"My mama said that you're gonna help save my life. Tell me you will, *please*. I love bein' alive and don't wanna go jus' yet."

Francine paused for a moment, studying the state of pain the poor girl was in, before responding. She wanted to tell her the truth and thus cleared her throat before speaking. "I will do my best, but almost all of it will depend upon you and whether you really want to be healed."

Mandi didn't respond.

Francine then proceeded. "Please, right this way."

She directed them to the outside patio located at the back of the house. There were two cushioned chairs that circled around a glass table that had a big umbrella hanging over it. Mandi was parked next to her mother who sat in one of the seats before shifting closer to her daughter. Francine approached them a few minutes later with a small leather briefcase.

As soon as she sat down, two maids brought assorted fruits and sandwiches over to them. Thelma had expected this, judging from the fact that it was the way in which all guests were treated under Francine's roof. The three of them began eating. Mandi could only eat small amounts, which she wished wasn't the case, since everything looked so good. Yet, she would eat the most she could. After about half an hour, they finished eating and the maids carried everything back to the kitchen so Francine could get started.

"Now… Mandi, my name again is Francine. I understand you're sick. You have cancer. Is that right?"

Mandi nodded.

"Well as you're mother said, I am here to help you get through this battle, which is to fight this disease so you will be finally healed from it and never have to be sick again. Now, would you like that?"

"Yes please," she nodded with joy.

"Okay, because first you're going to have to want to be healed before anything can take place. If you do as I suggest to the letter, I can almost guarantee you will be healed, *but* you must do as I suggest. If you're not willing to follow my instructions, than I wish you the best of luck and hopefully you find someone else that maybe could do a better job."

Mandi listened onward.

"I like your mother a whole lot and what she has meant to me and done for me over the years, which is why I'm doing this. So understand that you're in a very special place to be here today with me as I help reveal to you the information. But what you do with it is totally up to you. Do you understand?"

"Yes ma'am."

"Good. Now first of all, I want to make a few things clear. I am not a doctor. I have no medical training or license whatsoever. I never even took a class in medical school or anything like that. In fact, I never went to college. All I know is what works and what has been proven to work since the beginning of time. And the reason I know this is because it has helped my life tremendously, and has helped me obtain the things I have and continue to have to this day. So are you okay with that?

"Yes I am."

"Okay. After all, you put your life in the hands of a doctor already, and that didn't work out. So why not try a different approach? Hopefully, that makes sense."

Mandi nodded.

"Good now here we go. Now first off, do you believe you can be healed?"

Mandi stared at her without a response, which Francine noticed wisely.

"Okay let's backtrack. Do you *want* to be healed?"

"Yes."

"Well, then you must first believe you can be healed. It's through that belief that anything can ever start to happen."

Mandi stared at her closely.

Suddenly, Francine opened up her briefcase and brought out a book called, *The Science of Getting Rich* by Wallace D. Wattles, and opened up to a page to read aloud to Mandi.

"It says here in this book," Francine continued, "*Things are not brought into being by thinking of their opposites. Health is never to be attained by studying disease and thinking about disease; righteousness is not to be promoted by studying sin and thinking about sin; and no one ever got rich by studying poverty and thinking about poverty.*"

She then closed the book, putting it to the side.

"In other words, Mandi," Francine said. "You have to condition your mind differently by thinking of that which you want to happen rather than thinking of the opposite or at least dwelling upon it."

Francine then placed the book back in her briefcase before continuing on.

"The best way to explain this, Mandi, is this: We are all governed by one power at all parts of the globe. And that power binds you and I and everyone else on this planet. You can call it a frequency, or a force, or energy. You can even call it 'God' if you want. But I'm going to call it energy so that you understand better. We are connected by this energy that attracts and repels things in our lives based on our own thoughts. Basically, what that means is, that we attract into our lives whatever we think about most of the time. So therefore, if you think about money, you will attract money. If you think about better health, you will have better health. If you think about romance or a better relationship with your family, you will have those things. *And* if you think about the opposite of those things, you will attract them as well. It's all in your thinking. I'm willing to bet you that the reason you're in the health you're in now is because you adamantly thought about the disease whether consciously or unconsciously. Am I right?"

"Well... *maybe.*"

"There is no 'maybe' Mandi. You did. Now I know you may not have wanted to, but you did, which is why you're experiencing the pain and discomfort that you are in now. The doctor told you would die from the disease. And thus the symptoms perpetuated much faster because you believed it. You see, the energy of the universe will attract that into your life of what you think about most of the time. It doesn't know or care whether you're white or black, or went to college or didn't go to college, because it can't tell the difference. In addition, it doesn't recognize whether you want it or not. All it does is operate solely on your thoughts and emotions. It's a law. It's called the 'law of attraction.' And with that law, it states that like things attract other like things or something similar. Therefore, everything you have experienced in your life has been the direct result of your own thoughts, whether you realize it or not. Everything. Very few people understand or even know that. We are all the products of what we've thought about, 100 percent. Every credible philosopher throughout history has concurred to this fact. They may have disagreed on many other things, however, this law in particular is where they have all been in unanimous agreement. Buddha even confirmed it. He said, 'All we are, is what we've thought about.' So it's not a theory. It's a fact. It's just that not too many people know about it."

"But why?" asked Mandi.

"Well, that's a long story. But to put it in a nutshell, it's so that the powerful and elite class continue to have their control and power while the rest of the masses continue on as their servants. The elite do not want the masses to be exposed to this power and how to apply it because the elite would lose control. But that's neither here nor there for right now. The fact is that you're knowing this now. So all that's left is for you to know how to apply it."

"Well how do I do that?"

"First, you must think differently. You must think of all the things that you want and the universe will deliver it to you. No matter how great or how small the thought is, the universe will do everything in ensuring that you get that which you want. It will cut through buildings, trees, valleys, steel, mountains, rivers, oceans, waterfalls, and beyond to see that you get that which you want, which to the universe, was only because you thought about it."

Mandi was instantly excited. "Well, then how do I start thinking about being healthy?"

"Well first off, I'm going to give you a notebook for you to jot down all your dreams and goals, which I recommend that you do always with a blue pen. And what you should do is write down any and everything you want, no matter how big or small it is. Write down everything on paper to your heart's content. Even if it appears foolish, write it down. And Thelma, I would suggest that you don't help her. This is her own assignment and she should do it on her own. Do you understand?"

"Yes Francine, I do," Thelma replied. "But I just wanted to know, how come it has to be with just a blue pen? Why can't it be black or red or any other color?"

"Well without going into too much detail, blue ink that is written on a white piece of paper produces more clarity through the eyes of a person than any other color combination, which in effect sends a better signal or vibration for the universe to respond to. Don't ask me how it works. All I know is that this is what it does and it's what my mentor told me long ago."

"All right then. Fair enough," she answered.

Francine then continued on. "Secondly, Mandi, I want you to write down at least ten things you're grateful for. It can be your family or even meeting me. It can be anything. I want you to write them all down and look at it everyday, reading it to yourself. As you do this, more and more things you're thankful for will come to you, which you should write down. In fact from now on, I want you to carry your notebook wherever you go so if anything comes to mind, you can write it down. That will in turn change your thinking and help you to be more positive in your approach for better health."

"Thank you much ma'am," Mandi smiled.

"You're welcome. Well, that will be all for today. Here is your notebook and some blue pens to take along with you."

"Thank you."

"You're welcome... oh and before I forget. I want to lend you this book. It's about 20 years old but it's still as powerful as the day I first read it. It's called, 'The Magic of Believing' by Claude M. Bristol. It's a book that exposes the science of belief. I feel it will help you in understanding the power of thought in the mind and how to believe, which I think you'll grasp much quicker since you're really young... at only 12 years old."

"Thanks ma'am but I can't read that well."

"Well... do you have anyone in your family that can read to you?"

"Yes. I believe Carla, my sister can."

"Well have her read it to you. It doesn't have to be at one sitting. Just have her read as much as she can for that day or that hour and then have her read some more again some other time until she's done. But make sure she doesn't make the gap too long. Tell her that your life depends on it. If you say that, she'll listen."

Mandi smiled.

"Well Francine dear, I heard everything you said and learned so much myself. Thank you so much." Thelma said hugging her.

"You're welcome. You're both welcome, but it's far from over. She must first of all do the work."

"She'll do it. I'll make sure she does."

"Good thing."

"But Francine I want to tell you again that I appreciate having your time for today. We live in the South where it would be almost criminal for blacks and whites to get together this way. But you took it upon yourself to help us even though you've always had everything and never lacked a thing in yo' life. You still helped us get through. I am so grateful. You are a blessing to us all."

Francine smiled. "First of all I'm doing this because it was a promise I made long ago to my mentor, who has passed on now. I promised I would share this information with someone else regardless of creed, religion, nationality or the color of their skin, since it is a power that the whole world needs to know. Her dream was for the entire world to be educated on this secret and wanted me to carry on her dream. Second of all, it's very interesting to hear you say that I've always had everything. Well, let me tell you something about that. *Woman*, you have *no* idea about my full life story or what I've been through earlier in my life. Believe me, I know what it's like to suffer… and have nothing. But that's a good thing, because suffering makes you humble… like me. I just haven't told you my story yet. But in the near future, perhaps I will. Though for now, let's see what Mandi can do and hope she pulls through. Okay?"

"Fair enough."

"Good. Well okay, Mandi. It was nice to meet you. Since today is Thursday, you can all come back at one in the afternoon on Tuesday. That will give you a good amount of time to write your list, and maybe you can tell me how much you learned from the book Carla read to you, okay?"

"Yes ma'am," Mandi replied.

"All right, bye now."

"Bye."

One of the butlers then escorted Thelma and Mandi outside and Francine began waving to them while Mandi waved back, smiling. Suddenly, there was more than just hope. There was belief.

By the time Tuesday arrived, Mandi became eager to see Francine. She was so excited, accompanied by her mother, while carrying her notebook with such pride and enthusiasm.

"Good afternoon," greeted Francine waiting outside. "It seems we're all happy today."

"Yes ma'am," Mandi answered with joy.

"I can't wait to hear all about it. Come follow me."

They then arrived again at the back patio, where Mandi was full of joy. Francine also was excited for her. "So tell me. What did you do?" Francine inquired.

"Well first of all, I did what you said and wrote down all the things I'm grateful for. You want me to read it to you?"

"No that's all right. It's really not that necessary. As long that you did the exercise, it's quite all right for now. I just hope you read it to yourself everyday."

"I have and I made a list of the things I want. I want to be 100 percent healthy, that's number one. Number two is that I want to be able to go to school and finish college. I also want to finally catch a butterfly. Then I want to be a pediatrician, you know help out with the kids and stuff. Then I want to live to be 100 years old with lots of great-great grandkids. Then I want to go to Florida and visit Africa and see where my ancestors came from. Then I want to go to China and see ancient Egypt... "

"Wow, that's great Mandi," replied Francine. "It seems you're really getting the idea. That's wonderful."

Mandi had a long list. Thelma began to study it herself. "It doesn't say here that you want a man when you grow up though," she said suddenly.

"Mamuhh!"

"What? You ain't gone be a nun, is you?"

"But mama... "

"I'm jus' sayin'... If you want all dem dreams and goals, you gotta go all the way and be specific. You either do it right or don't do it at all. Just make sho' you put that down there somewhere... and you want him to be handsome, and real responsible and treat you nice, and won't cheat on ya when you're gone... "

"Mrs. Watkins, I'm sure she will figure all that out," concluded Francine, chuckling.

"Fair enough," she replied.

"Well that's good Mandi. I'm proud of you. Did your sister read to you?"

"Yes she did. Me and mama and papa heard her read and it was fantastic. I never knew the mind could do all that. It makes your thoughts become things."

"Your thoughts are things Mandi, and if you convince yourself that you are healthy, I guarantee you will be just that… healthy."

"Yes ma'am."

"Now what I want to discuss with you is something even more important. It has to do with your feelings. Your emotions play a huge role in getting what you want because it is the signal that tells the universe whether that which you're thinking of is what you really want. Therefore regardless of your circumstances, you must always form the habit of feeling good always… and feeling better. Now it is important that you make the decision and form it as a habit. That will then move you to the right track of what you want."

"Really?"

"Yes, really. To put it in simple terms, if you're desiring or thinking about having a nice bike and you're feeling good about having it, then that bike will eventually come into your life when you least expect it. But if you're thinking about a bike, but you're feeling bad about it, then that bike will never come into your life, because since your thought and feeling are not in alignment, they will thus repel your ability from having that bike."

"But even if I do all those things, which is think about it and feel good about it, how will it then come?"

"Well, basically the universe will put people, situations, events, and circumstances into your life to ensure you get that bike. You don't know how it's going to work and you shouldn't be concerned, because since you thought about that bike and feel good about that bike, you've already sent out a signal to the universe which will now make its own calculations, conducting millions of different variables in determining how best to bring that bike into your life. It may create a scenario of your next door neighbor wanting to move out and suddenly deciding to give their bike to your family since they feel they don't need it anymore. Or probably, you receive it as a surprise gift from a family member. Maybe, as you're walking down the street, you just happen to find it amongst some trash that some people just chose to throw away because they didn't want it any more. Or an opportunity may come for you to work in saving your allowance for the bike you want. Who knows and who cares. The fact is you've got what you want, and the possibilities are endless. But what is true is that at the right place at the right time, the universe will put certain people and situations in your life to ensure you receive that bike."

Instantly Mandi and Thelma got excited, smiling at each other. However Francine continued on. "Therefore the 'how' is not important. You leave that up to the universe or to God to figure that part out. It has already been determined 'how.' All you need to do is send out the signal, which is your thoughts and good feelings, and the universe will take it from there. It has to because it's a law. Got it?"

"Got it ma'am."

"Good. Even the late Einstein confirmed this, who by the way was the smartest man ever to live. Actually it was both him and Thomas Edison that believed this same principle. So it's not nonsense. Oh and by the way, you should never think negative thoughts, either."

"But how? Like sometimes, I find it hard not to think about this pain and how I cough all the time."

"Good. I'm glad you asked that. The most important thing you must master and practice everyday is to feel good. You must do that all the time, because as long as you're feeling good, it's impossible to think negative thoughts. The chemistry in your body just won't allow you. And actually, scientists say that we think more than 10,000 thoughts a day. So you shouldn't worry about every thought you're thinking. It's just the ones that you think of the most, which are most vital. But you have to always feel good. That's what tells you you're on the right track in attaining your goal."

Francine then caught her breath for a moment.

"Now, you shouldn't worry because I'm going to give you some instructions of things you must do to help you with your emotions. Here, look at this. It's a list of things you must do. I call it *my* prescription to you, which of course, you should use as directed."

Mandi took the paper and glanced at it. It read:

1. *Show gratitude everyday by saying the things you're thankful for*
2. *Read from your list the things you're thankful for*
3. *Always say positive and funny things to people and yourself*
4. *Try and crack good healthy jokes every once in a while*
5. *Laugh at least 20 minutes a day*
6. *Watch funny programs that make you laugh*
7. *Smile as often as possible*
8. *Eat raw fruits and vegetable as well as organic foods as much as possible everyday*
9. *Say aloud that you're so grateful for being healed as often as possible, everyday*

Francine then began explaining how each point was vital. She went on to say that expressions of gratitude help in developing the positive mindset of a person. She then said that the utterance of funny or positive things reflected the spirit of an individual, which the universe picks up tremendously. As for laughing, she explained that laughter causes alkalinity in the body in which disease can't exist and if a person laughs enough, he can actually reverse the entire physical process of the body, which can then form healthy cells, thereby eliminating the disease.

That in itself was something that made Thelma nearly fall out of her chair. She just couldn't believe something considered so minor, was so powerful. This was why Francine suggested that Mandi watch funny programs, because it was those programs that assisted with the laughter.

Francine emphasized that some diseases can be the result of nutritional deficiencies in the body. So according to her, it was important for Mandi to consume things that were as close as nature intended, primarily raw fruits and vegetables. By doing this, they would unleash natural properties that could assist with the repair of her body.

From observing people through the years, Francine believed that a person's state of health was determined largely by their lifestyle and eating habits more than anything else. Therefore, a person who was overweight and a heavy smoker was more likely to develop health problems than a person who wasn't. A little exercise, such as just walking for 30 minutes a day, could add tremendously to improving one's health. And really, Mandi wasn't to just do it after the healing process. She was to do it throughout her lifetime.

Francine also stressed to Mandi to eliminate any kind of meat from her diet, which in itself was a crushing blow to her and her mother. The entire Watkins family loved meat, especially chicken—and especially fried chicken—which was where they all grew off of. But to save her own life, Mandi was going to do exactly what her teacher advised, even though it appeared awfully hard. Simply put, if she wanted things in her life to change, she was going to have to change things in her life.

And as for number eight, here is what Francine said: "Mandi, you want to trick your mind and the universe in believing that you're already well because that is the signal that your brain is going to send out to the universe so that you become well. Remember, the universe can't determine whether you're really sick or not. All it does is respond to your feelings and thoughts and from there it sends out its command. So by acknowledging that you're healed already and grateful for it, you're expressing gratitude, which to the universe is exactly what you want: health. By doing this, you will help eliminate any worries, concerns, or fears you may have… which I'm sure you had before meeting me. Correct?"

"Yes, indeed," Mandi said with joy.

"Well good, because that changes today. Understood?"

"Yes ma'am."

"And if you want to just not worry about all those things, make a habit to feel good for 21 days and it will become a habit. From there, everything will just come to you automatically and naturally where fear or any negative emotion vanishes."

Thelma and Mandi were so thrilled. Their faces were so bright as if they had just come out of a vault with duffle bags of money.

Yet as further conversation ensued, Thelma informed Francine that they didn't own a television set. Francine then offered to loan her TV to them as long as Mandi promised to give it back once she got well. They both agreed and soon after, Francine called one of her men to bring a TV out for them, which had them both excited.

Programs that existed during those times were *The Three Stooges, Leave it to Beaver, The Andy Griffith Show,* and others that sent the funny but positive messages Francine encouraged Mandi to watch. Movies like *Gunsmoke* or films by John Wayne were not encouraged. Anything negative was completely unacceptable. Francine wanted to do none other than train Mandi's mind in the positive sense. She was to stay away from all negative ties whatsoever.

To further help Mandi form the habit of laughter, Francine lent her a couple joke books and suggested to Mandi that she allow Carla to read them aloud so as to get her in the laughing spirit. Some of the jokes contained in the books were really good, which Francine assured would cause her to have instant laughter beyond control.

Afterwards, Francine offered Mandi another book entitled, *The Power of Positive Thinking* by Norman Vincent Peale, which was to be completed after the first book was completely read out loud to her. In it, the author covered subjects almost parallel to what Francine discussed, but there were also subjects relating to health and its connection to human feelings, which were sure to help Mandi understand more about her recovery process.

When the session was finally over, Thelma called Charlie, who came over to pick up the TV. Afterwards, all three of them went home to begin the process.

5

⧽⧼

Mandi's Miracle

B Y THE TIME MANDI AND THELMA GOT HOME, THEY could no longer contain their excitement. They were thrilled with everything that Francine had told them thus far—and Mandi couldn't wait to put the lessons into practice. The feeling felt so exhilarating that instantly, Mandi finally believed in her heart that she could be healed.

Within the first week, Carla had finished reading aloud *The Magic of Believing* by Claude M. Bristol, and soon after read to Mandi *The Power of Positive Thinking* by Norman Vincent Peale. The book was phenomenal to Mandi. It automatically convinced her of the importance of feeling good all the time. Mandi carried a smile throughout the following day. She watched funny television programs, as Francine told her to, and gave updates on how things were going, which Francine adamantly wanted to know. Mandi did most of the things from the list that Francine gave her, while forgetting others.

However, Mandi eventually worked on the forgotten ones as well, remembering the attitude of not making excuses for not doing things. So she began remembering to tell herself: *Thank you Lord for healing me*. She tried her best to make it a habit to say it three times each morning, day, and before she went to bed.

As with the joke books, Carla read Mandi jokes from them from time to time, which caused her to laugh wildly. For instance, one read:

Question: When pastors want absolutely no noise during church offerings, what does that always include?

Answer: No sounds of coins jingling in their collection plate.

Apart from this, Francine also recommended that Mandi pray regularly to be cured. She couldn't emphasize enough the power of prayer. According to Francine, prayer carried tremendous power... *only and only when* it was attached to belief or 'faith' as all churches termed it. Mandi had to believe in what she was praying for—wholeheartedly—and then miracles would come into her life. And with the help of her mother, Mandi slowly began to form the habit of prayer. Thelma helped pray with her, along with the rest of the family.

Francine had also suggested that Mandi try to refrain from the many bottles of medicine, prescribed and not prescribed, by the doctor. To Francine, virtually all medications contained side effects of some sort that could alter the mood or emotions Mandi was supposed to have when feeling good. And when that happens, it keeps the body from being able to transmit positive vibrations effectively. Since positive outcomes only came from positive thoughts and emotions, it was important that the body stayed protected in a positive way at all times. And according to Francine, the lack of medications helped maintain such a habit.

Francine had to be careful because she didn't want such an opinion of hers to conflict with Mandi's doctor's, in turn getting condemned for giving 'bad' advice. So all Francine suggested to Mandi was that if she believed that the medications she was using were truly helping, then she should continue taking them, since it's the thoughts that made them so. But if she didn't feel any positive impact and rather, adverse side effects, then by all means, she should abandon such items immediately, and never use them again.

But only Mandi could make that call and no one else. It was her body. In the end, Mandi ceased from using her medications, since she felt the side effects all the time.

During this entire ordeal, Mandi began to challenge herself by trying to run along the sidewalk at full speed as a regular person would. She tried but fell several times. Darin, who had seen this, would help her up, reminding her that it doesn't come overnight. She just had to give it time, but should keep trying each day, never giving up. Along with these activities, Mandi began jumping rope with friends on a regular basis, along with playing hop scotch and riding a bike around the neighborhood.

She also listened to her favorite music played by artists such as Mississippi native Muddy Waters. Along with him, came music by Marvin Gaye, Ray Charles, The Temptations, and several others, which brought an instant smile to her face. She enjoyed listening to music—and dancing to it as well.

Within six weeks, she noticed that she began having a more positive outlook on life. She was always joyous, smiling. At times, she even forgot that she was sick. As time went on, she began noticing changes in her body she hadn't paid much attention to. The pains in her back and stomach weren't as severe, and she began noticing more of a comfortable feeling in her body as a whole. She could almost squat with ease or touch her toes without pain.

Mandi also ate farm-grown fruits and vegetables, and drank raw milk. Thelma started to bring her fruits and vegetables fresh from local farmers—just as nature intended. None of the crops that were sold in those markets had herbicides or pesticides in them.

Mandi also formed a habit to look at her goal book everyday, from which she kept changing her dreams from time to time. Francine had also suggested that Mandi cut out pictures from magazines and newspapers of healthy women. By doing this, it would create the picture in Mandi's mind of how she wanted to look. With the help of Thelma again, Mandi cut pictures from abandoned magazines she found and she smiled after pasting them to the pages of her notebook. Some of the pictures were even tacked to the walls of her room so that she could look at them before she went to sleep.

Soon, the affirmation of gratitude for being healthy became so profound for Mandi that she began to say it everywhere with such joy and enthusiasm. During that stretch, she discovered that her back and stomach pains had completely ceased, as well as the headaches. She suddenly was able to walk a mile without grimacing even once. She rarely even coughed, and was hardly ever tired. In fact, her siblings were surprised because whenever everyone wanted to go to sleep, Mandi couldn't stop running her mouth about everything that went on in school and throughout the day.

Her teacher even commended Charlie and Thelma on Mandi's improved grades, claiming that she had such renewed vigor and excitement. The observation nearly brought Thelma to tears.

After about six months since Mandi's first visit with Francine, nearly every facet of her physical attitude changed. Previously, anyone who had seen her not even for a minute on the street could tell that she was 'sick.' Her siblings even began to wonder if she was at all cured in any way because their sister was rarely showing any signs other than those of a normal 13-year-old. They soon began to get very curious to find out what exactly was going on, especially since Mandi supposedly should have 'died,' according to the doctor.

Within a few weeks, the siblings gathered together and asked Thelma if she could take Mandi to the doctor to determine if there were any improvements in her condition. Thelma, a little nervous, began to feel it wasn't necessary, for fear that the doctor would report another problem. To Thelma, since Mandi appeared healthy, there was no reason to have a doctor say it. However, the siblings insisted that their mother still find out, suggesting that it would be nothing other than just his opinion.

Thelma eventually gave in and took Mandi to go see the doctor. The doctor, who was a bit surprised by Mandi's return, took her blood and made a few scans before suggesting that they return the following week for the results. The doctor asked Thelma if Mandi was still taking her medications.

Thelma lied and said that she was (since she didn't want to hear the doctor's mouth), saying of how necessary it was for Mandi to take them.

When Thelma and Mandi arrived the next week, they were told that the results were not ready yet, and to come back next week. The following week, Thelma received the same news, that the results were not complete. Thelma began to get a little hot-tempered and wondered what was going on. Mandi also wanted to know.

Now it had been a month since Mandi had her last evaluation. So Thelma instinctively bypassed the front counter, rushed through the hallway to check the room where Dr. Spencer was, found the door and immediately stormed into his office, which startled him.

"How come you keep delaying on telling us Mandi's results?" she demanded.

Just then, a security officer, a desk clerk, and two nurses arrived behind her. Dr. Spencer, who suddenly realized what was going on, suggested that the security officer and clerks leave while he and Thelma talk. So they left. Thelma remained at the door.

Dr. Spencer removed his glasses after reviewing a few slides before directing her to his other office. He had his hands on his waist, appearing nervous and unaware of how to begin. He suddenly began to stutter, as he was trying to talk; an attitude he rarely ever expressed before.

"Well... the reason I... I couldn't... give... give you the results yet, is because... because my colleagues and I are still scratching our heads... trying to figure out what happened. We tried comparing the most recent results from the ones seven months ago and they seem totally... *different*; like night and day. I've never seen anything like it. And the reason I couldn't release them was because my colleagues... and I... were trying the best way we could to explain just what happened, but... we still can't. So I might as well tell you now and get it all over with."

"What is it?" she demanded.

"Well, uh Mrs... Mrs... uh... "

"Watkins. Thelma Watkins."

"Yes that's right. Thelma. Thelma Watkins. Well Thelma, the truth is that somehow her cancer... and mind you, this is strange saying this, but her cancer went into... complete remission, totally. I can't figure out how it happened. In all my years of practice, I have never... "

"Doc, now you lis'en tuh me. I nevuh went to high school much less college. So you're gonna have to explain it in plain English that even my youngest child, Rosaline can understand. *Please*, can you do that fo' me? I'm not used to all dem big words. I mean what do *remission* mean, by you sayin' it's complete and all? I mean what dat mean?"

"Sure... uh, what that means is that she's... and you're going to have a hard time believing this, but she's... cuh... cc-*cured*. She's free from any deadly cancer. She's cancer free. Congratulations."

Almost instantly, Thelma jumped up from her chair, ran over to hug the doctor, saying: *"Thank you Jesus! Oh thank you, God!"* Without really knowing how to act, Thelma kissed Dr. Spencer on the cheeks, which had him scared and frightened for some reason. The real question, according to him, was, what did Thelma do to Mandi or what did Mandi do to herself to be cured? The doctor didn't know the answer, which made him think that Thelma was a witch of some sort.

He wanted to conduct another test on Mandi, but saying that would have probably brought an outrage by her family, thereby questioning his competence.

"I guess the medications finally helped, huh?" he suddenly alleged.

"Whatevuh doc. *Whatevuh*," Thelma responded with tears in her eyes. After hugging him, she shook his hands, and said "thank you."

"But please be advised, I'm going to have to bill you for this visit," added Dr. Spencer, quickly.

But it was too late. Thelma was already gone, off to tell everyone the good news.

When the entire family heard it, everyone was ecstatic. Mandi was almost in tears. Francine had definitely saved her life. Any and everything she had ever said worked. At that moment, Mandi wanted to rush to the nearest pay phone to tell Francine, but Thelma stopped herself dead in her tracks, indicating that they were going to do it the right way.

Thelma decided to bake Francine a delicious cake, which she was going to love along with a dozen roses to complement it.

Thelma was an expert at baking cakes and so she knew exactly the type of cake that was Francine's favorite. Francine was an avid lover of cheesecake. And Thelma had the secret recipe she formed herself to make the most delicious cheesecake. It was going to be rich and creamy and unforgettable.

She went and got all the ingredients from the grocer and she and Mandi chose to work together to make it. Thelma was going to share with Mandi her secret recipe, which she had never shared before with anyone. She didn't even want her other children to know. To Thelma, what she gave Mandi was something so special that she figured only Mandi deserved. In return, Mandi promised to never tell anyone about the recipe.

After a few hours, they pulled the cake out of the oven and it smelled so delicious. Thelma and Mandi smiled at each other. Mandi started to use her index finger to take a sample, but Thelma instantly slapped her hand.

"Ouch!" reacted Mandi.

"We'll all find out when we get to her house," reminded Thelma while taking a sample of her own.

"I just had to make sho'. That's all," she said. "Now let's put it in the box."

Both of them carefully carried the cake before placing it in a cardboard box. They then carried the box and put it in the bag. After a while, the two of them got dressed. Thelma wore her beautiful church outfit along with a matching hat. Mandi wore a long brown skirt and a black short-sleeved blouse before putting on her black dress shoes. She was beautiful. It was at this moment Thelma suddenly recognized how beautiful her daughter really was.

Mandi was light-skinned with a semi-flat nose. She had full lips and brown eyes. Her teeth were a bright white that could light up any room whenever she smiled. At age 13, her other features were not yet developed, but anyone looking at her could easily tell that she would grow up to become a very attractive young lady. Even Thelma knew it. All the boys were going to go wild if not already, she thought.

"You look gorgeous, baby," Thelma commended, almost in tears.

Mandi smiled, shifting sideways. "Thank you ma."

Thelma then went up to fix Mandi's collar. "Now come on child. Let's go see that spiritual healer of ours." Thelma smiled, while taking Mandi by the hand.

"Yes *ma'am*," replied Mandi.

Thelma almost couldn't believe this was her daughter. What a difference six months makes.

"Just don't fo'get the roses," she reminded. "I'll carry the cake... with the card."

"Okay."

From there, the two of them were off. Francine on the other hand, wasn't expecting anybody or anything. She was actually reading while they were coming, unaware of even the good news the doctor had given. Therefore, this was all going to be a big surprise.

Minutes later, she heard a call from one of the maids for her to come down. Francine began thinking that it was a particular man whom she told earlier not to return. So without knowing who it was, Francine wiped her face, combed her hair and rushed down to tell that same salesman not to ever come by her property again. She jokingly thought of grabbing a shotgun to make the message clear.

But upon approaching the entranceway, she was immediately stunned to see Mandi and Thelma before her. Instantly, she smiled.

"Oh... oh my gosh. I... I thought you were someone else."

Thelma and Mandi just looked at her and smiled.

"Well, what are you women doing here? I mean what seems to be the occasion?"

"You saved my life!" Mandi shouted. "The doctor said I'm cured!"

Francine was shocked. "Oh... really?"

"Yeah and me and my mama made a special cheesecake and here are some roses."

Francine was immediately out of words. She didn't know what to say. A part of her knew it would happen, yet a part of her still couldn't believe it. She was officially a spiritual healer. She covered her mouth with both hands almost in total disbelief.

Thelma spoke. "Thank you boss. We all love you. It's now I found out that there's good in all people no matter the color of their skin." Suddenly Thelma began to break down in tears. "*You saved my daughter's life,*" she cried. "*You don't know how much this means tuh me. It's a miracle! Thank you so much.*"

One of the maids went quickly over to collect the box before it fell from Thelma's hands, which gave her an easy chance to hug her employer and savior. "I love you Francine," she said, hugging her. "I really do love you."

Francine then looked in her eyes. "Listen, don't you cry. I love you too." Soon, she too began to get emotional herself, wiping her wet eyes.

"Please let's all go to the kitchen and eat some cake," she said.

Within minutes, the three of them were all together enjoying each other having a good time. Francine was so delighted with the cake, she almost couldn't contain herself. "This is the best cake I have ever eaten. Thank you so much. I needed this. Where'd you get it?"

"I made it," Thelma answered.

"*We* made it," corrected Mandi suddenly.

"Yes child, we made it all right."

"So I guess it's *your* little secret, huh?" questioned Francine.

"I guess so," Thelma replied.

Francine, who was now looking at both of them carefully, eventually got the idea. "Well, if ever I want another cake, I won't mind calling either of you to make me one, *which* I will gladly pay for."

"Good enough," said Thelma.

As soon as they were done, Francine composed herself before suggesting that they all meet at the back patio again. The three of them went there, where Thelma, as usual, sat closer to Mandi, while Francine sat in front of them at the table. Though it was such a delight to see that, rather than seeing Mandi in a wheelchair. Mandi was perfectly comfortable sitting in a patio chair all by herself.

Suddenly out of nowhere, a butterfly came whirling around them before landing on the table, near Mandi's hand. Then it fluttered in the air and landed on her index finger. Mandi, surprised by all this, carefully raised the butterfly with her index finger, and looked at it closely. Ironically, the butterfly didn't flinch even for a moment. It just stayed on her finger calmly, trusting that it was already safe.

Francine and Thelma, who saw this, were both marveled. Mandi of course couldn't believe it. She wanted to cry, surprised at how naturally the butterfly came to her. Then, after about a few minutes, the butterfly flew away, which left everyone stunned.

After a brief moment, Francine then began the conversation. "So how do you feel?" she asked Mandi.

"Amazing!" she exclaimed.

"Good, I'm happy to hear that. In fact, I'm glad you both came. I don't have anything else scheduled or planned for this afternoon except my routine walk later on. So I feel now would be the perfect time to tell my story about when I was your age, Mandi. That way, you know that life for me at first wasn't at all easy either. I suffered too."

"Okay," she replied.

"Thelma, are you ready darling, to hear where your boss once was?"

"Yes ma'am. Preach!"

"Okay, here goes."

Francine was born into a poor Irish family, known as the 'Sullivans,' who emigrated from Ireland to America, initially settling in Brooklyn, New York before moving to Virginia. She was the oldest child in her family, where they lived in a dirty one-bedroom shack. The floor of their home was filled with dirt, covered with hay. Her father, a former bootlegger, later became an alcoholic; her mother was a seamstress. Life was so rough growing up. Francine would walk a half a mile down the road every other day, carrying branches of firewood for cooking and pails of water for the house, while her father, Paul, did business back in New York, conducting bootlegging operations, which were very lucrative at the time.

Their home had only one bedroom, which had an uneven floor, where Francine, along with her four siblings, slept. There were no beds with thick sheets for them to lay their heads on. The clothes they wore were always dirty and torn, and each child only owned three pairs of clothes. Occasionally, there was not enough food to eat, which caused a lot of sickness in the home.

In fact it was the result of sickness that led to the death of her youngest brother, Samuel, who died in Francine's arms of polio at the age of two. Francine, who was devastated, blamed herself for quite some time. It was a horrible experience for her, and it made her shed tears whenever she remembered that time. Coupled with this was the lack of money, which forced her and her brothers, Walter and Josh, to steal food from local people's farms and beg for money on the streets. Her mother, who was a seamstress, had lost her job a few years before the Great Depression, and became depressed of her inability to support her children.

During this time as well, her father spent four months in jail for affiliation in bootlegging, which caused further depression in the household. When he was released however, he was fired from his bootlegging job and the embarrassment and failure that he had put his family through consumed him to the point that he chose alcohol, and he began drinking non-stop as a "safe haven" from his shame. This in turn affected his marriage to Francine's mother. They constantly argued, forcing each of them to become miserable.

Mildred was a miserable unemployed mother with four people to support, while her husband could do nothing but drink himself to death. Francine's father always focused on Mildred's failures, complaining when she never prepared supper or did the laundry. Throughout the night, Francine and her siblings would hear the loud commotions and screams echoing between her parents non-stop until she cried herself to sleep.

Her brothers and sister, Annie, found no choice but to lean on Francine for support, thinking that she was the wisest person left in the family. But Francine was no stronger than they were. She was constantly annoyed with everything that went on. She was tired of being hungry, tired of the verbal attacks and almost tired of even being alive. She wished she could just run away and abandon her family. Yet it was only the concern for her siblings that kept her from going anywhere.

As fate would have it however, a small fight between Francine and Mildred erupted, which forced Francine to go to the store alone early one morning. On her way there, Francine saw a vehicle coming head on toward a young girl, which caused Francine to instinctively sprint to save the child from being hit. This in turn was what led her to meet Mary Jo, the girl's mother. Mary Jo had her arms full of grocery bags as she crossed the street, and her daughter had halted in the middle of the road, which made Mary Jo unable to pull her away in time.

Stunned by Francine's remarkable heroism, Mary Jo decided to expose the secret to her as payment. Mary Jo gave Francine the address to her luxurious estate where she would then teach her about the law of attraction. Upon teaching it, she gave Francine books written about the power of the mind and how things came into one's existence through thoughts. It was then that Francine became so fascinated with reading, that she read, *As a Man Thinketh* by James Allen over a dozen times. Along with this, she read: *The Science of Getting Rich* by Wallace D. Wattles and *Acres of Diamonds* by Russell H. Conwell; all of which Mary Jo lent her to read.

During their initial conversation, Francine eventually told Mary Jo that she desired a rich husband who would have the positive qualities that she desired in a man. Mary Jo then told her to write it down in her dream book and look at it every day, believing it would come true.

During this time, Francine began to develop a positive attitude at home and most of the fights between her mother and father suddenly ceased, at least while she was there. She eventually got a job and was able to support part of her family's needs. She also bought herself a few new outfits so that she could dress well wherever she went.

She eventually received from Mary Jo the voluminous book by Napoleon Hill called *The Law of Success in Sixteen Lessons*. In that were virtually all the elements of success that Napoleon uncovered after interviewing 500 of the richest and most successful men and women of his time to discover the principles that made them all successful. Francine became engrossed with the book and began modeling the elements described in it, which fully revealed her positive nature.

Then one day, while reading *As a Man Thinketh* again, while in town a young man named John Williamson suddenly approached her to find directions to a hardware store on behalf of his father who wanted to remodel a guesthouse. Francine gave the correct directions and the young man later returned back to continue talking with her. Their small talk led to dinner that same day. John, who was so amazed and impressed by how Francine carried herself, decided to get to know her better. He eventually surprised her with flowers and further dating ensued. Soon, he decided to invite her to his father's estate to introduce her to him.

His father was adamantly opposed to Francine because of her poor background, and warned John that if he ever married her, he would cease to ever claim him as his son. John in response, said: 'Amen. Amen. *So shall it be,*' and he left the house with Francine to propose marriage that same evening.

Upon discovering her wish had come true, Francine said: *"Oh John, I will not only marry you, but I assure you that I will remain faithful and loyal to you for as long as I live. I will diligently be an exceptional wife and good mother. This I promise you… always. So yes, I will. I will!"*

John couldn't have been more pleased. During that same night, they went together to inform her parents. Months later at only 19, Francine walked down the aisle in a stunning wedding dress. The wedding was held in an open field of a Catholic Church. It was the most magical moment of her life.

Yet, in order to avoid his father and other negative people around them, John chose for the both of them to move to Mississippi and build a luxurious estate, which was now where Francine, Thelma and Mandi were sitting. Though before Francine left Virginia, Mary Jo instructed her to tell the secret to someone else. Mary Jo told her that she had often envisioned how the world would be if everyone was exposed to the information and hoped Francine would pass that message along, thus keeping the dream alive.

Mary Jo said: "Now I don't know what you're going to be doing in Mississippi and it's quite possible that I may never see you again. But I beg that you take heed to my request. Remember everything I taught you. Encourage the person to read books and tell your story, and then once that person has received their miracle, you encourage that same person to share it with someone else they don't know, and in time, this world will change for the better. And that's really how change begins. It all starts with one step. And now that step is you."

When Francine said that she would share it, Mary Jo immediately made it clear that the person could be anyone, regardless of creed, nationality, race or gender.

"If you haven't noticed, we all are one," Mary Jo told her. "There is no separation of man but the ones we establish in our own minds."

That quote stuck with Francine and she promised wholeheartedly to share it. Over the years while Francine was in Mississippi, she and Mary Jo continued to keep in contact through letters. Mary Jo insisted that she get photos of Francine and her family, because Mary Jo wanted to frame them as a memory of the impact she had on Francine's life. Francine did, and the two of them continued their friendship.

By the time Francine turned 45, Mary Jo had died. She was 72. Then, five years later, Francine's husband and best friend, John, died. Francine remained confident that she would still find someone to mentor; and soon, that dream finally came true. She found Mandi. And now it would be *her* turn to share the secret with someone. However, Francine never encouraged Mandi share the secret right away, but to at least think about the idea when she got older.

When Francine was done telling her story, she slowly drank her glass of freshly squeezed orange juice. Mandi and Thelma were in a state of awe over the story. Never in a million years would Thelma have ever guessed that such was Francine's past.

"Now my mentor has passed on, but I still carry her dream to this day. Nothing would make me prouder than to see that same dream of hers fulfilled through someone else and that it can help create a better planet and better world for all mankind, especially since I know now that I also won't be here forever."

There was a pause. "I'll be the one," Mandi uttered spontaneously.

Francine smiled. "Are you sure?"

"Yeah, I know a whole bunch of people that need to know."

"Well in truth dear, everyone needs to know. However, you must not play with this, because this is not a joke. It's a job that must be taken seriously with responsibility and commitment."

"I know. I'm committed. I'll do it," Mandi confirmed again.

Francine smiled. "Well child, you're 13 years old. You have a whole life ahead of you. The most important thing now is that you finish school and go on to college. Then possibly, when you're ready, we'll talk about it. As for now, just enjoy being the healthy 13-year-old girl that you are. In time, the opportunity will present itself, just like the opportunity came for me to hire your mother, who later led me to you."

"Well I'm telling you Francine," Thelma interrupted, "you don't have to worry about any of that. I will make sure that she accomplishes the mission. As she's saying it now, I'll see to it that she does it."

"Well that's good. But before we close, I want you all, especially you, Mandi, to remember something very important. You know now that this secret is extremely powerful and can grant you anything you wish. But at the end of the day, it isn't what you have that's most important—it's the person you become. When we leave this world, the question at the end of the day will not be how much money we made… because we can't take it with us. The real question will be: Did we matter? And if so, who did we affect? That's the real question. Everything else is meaningless. See, when you're able to impact lives of people around you just as you were impacted, that tells more about you as a human being than anything else in the world. Mary Jo told me this and it isn't until now that I truly understand. So… it's something I pass onto you to think about."

Both Thelma and Mandi were in deep thought from that statement.

"Well ladies, I really had fun today. Again, thank you both for the cheesecake. It was *fabulous!* But I have to do my routine walk for the day."

"No thank *you* for everything you've done," replied Thelma. "May God keep you on this earth as long as you wish, inspiring others like you inspired me and my daughter. We will never ever forget this moment. Thank you so very much."

"You're welcome but remember… if you really want to thank me, just think about what I said and hopefully, you'll do it as well. Just pay it forward."

"I will," Mandi said quickly.

Francine looked at her closely. "That's my girl," she cheered. "For knowledge to ever be kept, it must be shared."

Eventually, all three ladies rose up from the chairs hugging one another. Afterwards, Thelma and Mandi were escorted out. In a few months, Mandi would turn 14 and high school would begin.

6

✥

Adolescence

M ANDI WAS NOW IN THE NINTH GRADE AT AGE 14. SHE was so excited. To her, beginning high school on her own was an accomplishment in itself, judging from the fact that she wasn't *supposed* to have made it that far. So she felt blessed.

Since Carla first read her the book *The Magic of Believing* by Claude Bristol, Mandi suddenly had a desire for learning. She just wanted to know more about different topics. That book, coupled with other books that Francine had recommended, intrigued Mandi so much that she asked Francine for more books to read that were among the same topics as the previous books. Francine had no problem with that.

Apart from *The Magic of Believing* and *The Power of Positive Thinking* by Norman Vincent Peale, Mandi was also lent *Psyco-cybernetics* by Maxwell Maltz. The book was more in depth about the brain and its capabilities and how it plays in proportion with attitude. There were so many elements in the book that it took Mandi a good month to absorb it. Soon after, Francine awarded Mandi another book through Thelma called *The Magic of Thinking Big* by David J. Schwartz. It was another book on attitude and touched on almost every cylinder of personality that a person must improve upon in order to become a more positive and successful human being. Mandi just loved both books.

Originally, she was not a good reader, but after patience and consistency and help from her sister Carla, Mandi improved dramatically and could read and pronounce almost every English word under the sun. She was familiar with vowels and consonants, and the different sounds they made. Therefore, even if the words were of a foreign language, she could still pronounce them almost perfectly without knowing what they even meant.

In high school, she became an exceptional student, always making grades that were at least a 'B' or above. Thelma was elated. Mandi later finished ninth grade with flying colors. Her favorite subjects were reading, science and history. She was not that big of a fan of math, but did well in it anyway, which made it hard to tell why she didn't like it. With history, she loved facts and was thrilled to find out about events that led up to the present day.

After reading the last two books of Francine's, Mandi became so intrigued with the human mind that by age 15 she had decided to become a psychologist. She still wrote in her dream book, later crossing out her initial dream of becoming a pediatrician. By this time, her dream book was worn out as a result of using it so much, so she transferred all the contents from her old book into a new one.

Midway through the tenth grade, Mandi had her sights on a boy. He was of brown complexion, and was in all of her classes. His name was Fletcher. Fletcher Campbell. He was about 5'9 and at 175 pounds had quite a good build, which

Mandi had her eyes on all the time. Fletcher knew this all too well.

He played basketball for their school where he was a starting guard. He also ran track and tried once to engage in football but ended up quitting, claiming it was too rough. He also dabbled in a little boxing and played some soccer, thus making him an all-around athlete. He was the third of six children. His father had been in prison after assaulting his mother, leaving Fletcher, his five siblings and mother to fend for themselves. However, since his parents were never married, his mother had a live-in boyfriend who treated her for the most part as family, as well as the children. Yet for Fletcher, the thought of living in that home without his father was difficult to swallow. Therefore, when he found himself at odds with the *other* man and his mother, he would just leave the house to catch some fresh air, to avoid entering into a physical altercation. He knew his limits.

He was not as good in his scholastic subjects as he was in sports, which was where Mandi came in. Fletcher knew Mandi liked him—and he liked her. Not long after, the two of them became affectionate and would hang out often, usually after school. Soon, Mandi began to feel that she was in love with Fletcher, so she made a point to add a new goal to her book: that she wanted to marry Fletcher.

It occurred all too suddenly, but judging from the fact that he was her first boyfriend and first love, the universe had to definitely make it happen… so she thought. Throughout the course of her life since her recovery, Mandi had continued to stay positive, both mentally and emotionally. Seldom did anything worry her and she always had a sense of hope, showing gratitude for the day. So in her mind, the universe gave her someone to be happier about, and that was Fletcher.

Soon she began dreaming of how things would be if they were married. She would become this renowned psychologist, while he played professional ball. They would have children and a house with white picket fences—the typical American Dream. At times, she attended some of Fletcher's games. He was an exceptional basketball player and the best player on the school team, averaging 16 points a game, 5 rebounds and 6 assists. So the thought of having a shot at professional ball wasn't too far fetched. All he had to do was get better grades in his junior and senior years and he could probably take a shot at some major college to show the nation his talent. And, she thought, if he could grow a little taller, that would also be a definite plus.

As months passed, it didn't take long for the thought of sex to enter their minds. Mandi, who was both nervous and anxious, immediately confided in her sister Carla. Carla promptly gave Mandi some condoms, to have with her whenever she was with Fletcher and also recommended that Mandi never have sex unless he was wearing one.

Mandi took her advice and presented one to Fletcher while in his mother's house. He put it on and the two of them made love. It was Mandi's first time. By now she was 16. It later became so enjoyable that Carla literally had to give Mandi several condoms to last quite a while. Later on, after one session, Mandi looked into Fletcher's eyes and smiled: "Fletcher. Do you love me?"

Fletcher thought for a moment. "Yeah… I… I… I… lo… ove you," he answered.

Fletcher wasn't at all confident. Yet, Mandi took his word and kissed him on the lips.

Throughout her junior year, Mandi continued to excel in school, and became one of the top 10 students in her class. She took a few honors courses, where she still did well, not skipping a beat. She was disciplined. In other words, when it came to academics, Mandi did not play around. Absolutely nothing came between her and her schooling.

When summer finally came around, Mandi finished with flying colors again, earning nothing but 'A's on her report card. The entire family was happy, especially Thelma, who cried when seeing the results, giving her daughter a great big kiss before serving a delicious plate of the signature cheese-cake.

Soon after, Mandi chose to surprise Fletcher by going to his house to celebrate both the good news about her grades, and to just hang out. When she got there, she wanted to knock on the door, but hesitated. She realized the front door was already cracked open, so she decided to just step in, as she had done in the past. As soon as she entered, she noticed two pairs of shoes just inside the door, one that appeared to be Fletcher's and another that obviously belonged to a girl.

Suddenly she heard noises. Mandi, a bit anxious and scared, instantly followed the direction of the noise and opened a bedroom door, only to find Fletcher on top of some other girl. Fletcher instantly turned around and covered himself in sheets, while the other girl immediately covered her chest. At first glance, Mandi knew who it was. Then she looked at Fletcher, and in a split second ran out of the house screaming in tears. Fletcher, who tripped and stumbled in a blanket while trying to chase her to offer some sort of expla-nation, suddenly stopped when he reached the doorway to the house. Mandi was nowhere in sight. She was long gone.

After running a couple blocks, she then went into a park-ing lot beside a brick building, crying like never before. She was so angry and upset. What made it worse was that the girl who Fletcher was with was Judi Hall, Mandi's supposed best friend. Throughout her relationship with Fletcher, Mandi had told Judi a lot about Fletcher and how in love she was with him. Though little did Mandi know, Judi had used those conversations as a green light to find out for herself about this boy. Mandi thought that best friends tell each other ev-erything. She was sadly mistaken.

A key rule Mandi was now learning was that most wom-en like a challenge and usually want what they can't have. It was a test of their perseverance and strength and, of course, what they could get out of it. Mandi was so heartbroken and did not want to hear from Fletcher again. But in truth, since he was a basketball star, Fletcher flirted and had affairs with several women. It's just that Mandi was so in love with him that she was oblivious to the warning signs before her.

For the next few days, Mandi was depressed, telling her family what had happened. To her, she just couldn't figure it out. How could the universe respond this way when she had nothing but high spirits and was so full of joy? It just didn't make sense. If you feel good, you're supposed to get good results, aren't you?

Not long after, Thelma brought Mandi over to Francine's house to explain the situation. Thelma tried to explain in the best way she could, but Mandi wanted clearer answers from Francine. And Thelma had no problem with that. Thelma was far from proud, and would always ask for help if she didn't know the answer.

When Mandi tried explaining to Francine what had happened, Francine was very attentive, listening patiently before trying her best to respond.

According to Francine, the universe did nothing wrong having Mandi experience what she had with Fletcher, since that was a sign that he wasn't the right match for her. To Francine, man can't compete with the universe in knowing what's best for him, since the universe knows more than what man sees. Mandi may have thought that Fletcher was the right one for her, but to the universe, that wasn't the case, and thus it was sending Mandi a signal to discover things earlier on before going any further down an unknown path. From Francine's point of view, Mandi instantly fell in love with Fletcher, and didn't listen to the warning signs that the universe was trying to send out. And this was the key to finally paying attention.

To help her understand, Francine told the story of her nearly four-year ordeal wishing for a rich husband. In her dream book, Francine wrote that she wanted a rich man who was God-fearing, loving, caring, compassionate and some other positive qualities. And from there, she began dreaming for such a man to appear while improving her attitude. After applying the said techniques for a couple years, she began to get a bit frustrated and asked her mentor, Mary Jo, why such a man hadn't come into her life.

Mary Jo answered, explaining that Francine needed to have patience and believe that such a man was coming her way. Mary Jo then went on to say that from the feelings and wishes that Francine was sending, the universe was factoring in millions upon millions of different variables that were all connected to each other before sending that wish she sought into her existence. She continued to say that it would require a bit more time and patience to find that which she seeks, but if she starts to doubt, then the effort the universe has put in would suddenly dissipate, since it's adhering to her command, which is doubt.

The reason this is so is because when one doubts, the thoughts one originally intended become less and less frequent, which are the signals the universe needs to continue to operate on the original command.

Mary Jo later added that just as a pregnant woman waits for a baby, and a student waits for his degree, both cases require time to develop, just as the universe needs time to develop its manifestations. And if Francine wasn't patient and suddenly forced herself upon someone, thinking that it was just 'time,' then she might get married but would never truly be happy, since that husband of hers could suddenly reveal himself as having qualities that were the opposite of what Francine had wished for.

This doesn't mean that the law of attraction doesn't work, it's just that Francine signaled impatience, which ties to worry and fear of the original intention, thereby bringing into her life what she didn't want. According to Mary Jo, if Francine exemplified complete calmness and faith in her goals, the right person would come into her life naturally, and Francine would know instantly without much effort. She would just know.

So afterwards, Mary Jo encouraged Francine to continue to read books while awaiting her husband. And as fate would have it, a man in a luxury car soon pulled up to her while she was reading in town, requesting directions. Francine closed her book and answered the man, and their eyes connected, and they instantly knew that they each had what the other needed. Then, about six months later, the young man proposed, and they were married months later. And mind you, her husband, John Williamson, still married her despite his father's violent opposition to it. Such true love could have only occurred through patience and the power of the universe. No other thing could explain it. What other hold could Francine have had on John if it wasn't through that? After all, she was a poor girl.

So what Francine advised is that though this may be a hard challenge for Mandi to endure, she should be thankful anyway, forgetting all that had happened, believing that the universe is steering her in the right direction, will bring her long-standing joy and happiness in the future instead of pain. If she was patient and just sent out positive thoughts of what she wanted in a man, then that perfect someone will eventually appear in her life when she least expected it—and she will know automatically.

And on a final note, Francine told Mandi that as long as she continued to remain positive, whatever may appear as an obstacle or hindrance will eventually reveal itself and go in her favor, and that later down the road, perhaps she'll discover why Fletcher wasn't the one for her.

After hearing that, Mandi and Thelma hugged Francine tight, thanking her for the explanation. Francine then revealed to Mandi that she should never again tell anyone her goals. They should remain private, always.

It should be indicated however, that while Mandi was busy writing down her own goals back when she was sick, she should have also listened to her mother's advice. Thelma was correct in telling her the type of man she should wish for. Since Thelma had her moments when she appeared to sound more humorous than sensible, Mandi often ignored her. But she now discovered that Thelma was right all along.

When Mandi got home, she did the exercise and listed that she wanted a man who was loyal, honest, considerate, caring, loving, supportive, responsible and God-fearing. There were other similar attributes she described as well. As far as physical appearance, she desired a man who was healthy and slim. And being good looking wasn't bad, either. (After all, she didn't want ugly children.)

Before her senior year began, Thelma made a transition of her own. As a matter of fact, it was big. She decided to quit working for Francine and finally start her own cake company. It had been a dream Thelma had before even meeting Charlie. However, she hadn't the mental tools or belief she could do it. But thanks to Francine showing her the gift of the mind and how to apply the law of attraction, Thelma took a leap of faith and decided to just get it done.

She got some books and began learning how the business worked from other bakery owners. With some money saved along with Charlie's, she felt she had enough to at least start. Now because this was the first time Thelma owned any kind of business, naturally she didn't know how any of this was going to turn out. All she knew was that she was doing something she had always wanted to do and that her whole family could be proud of her and feel inspired; and they would know that they could do anything they set their minds on, too. Besides, Thelma had gotten a lot of praise from family and relatives who all loved her cakes, and she felt that by stay-ing in the community, she had a lot of support.

When Francine first heard the news, she was a little shocked, but in the end, she was happy for Thelma and gave her her blessing. From the bottom of Francine's heart, she wished Thelma the best and promised her that she could al-ways come back if she ever desired. A close bond had been built between them through the years and Francine was go-ing to miss Thelma. Yet still, she was happy that Thelma had finally realized her calling.

Thelma eventually called the bakery *Thelma's Secret*. Thelma would have help from Carla and Darin, who would assist with the daily routine in running the bakery—a perfect decision since they were family. Both siblings were excited to help their mother. They now had something to call their own.

Mandi returned to the 12th grade energized. She was still a bit shaken by what had happened a few months prior, but tried her best not to think about it, which in time didn't take long. Surprisingly, Fletcher never returned back to school for his senior year. No one knew where he was, and assumed he just moved someplace else, which relieved Mandi a great deal while trying to get over him.

As far as Judi was concerned, she was said to be pregnant by another guy and therefore wanted to forgo her senior year in order to avoid the risk of distraction and embarrassment while attending school. So, the plan was for her to finish high school the following year after she had her baby. Plus, she didn't want to see Mandi's face. The idea of being looked upon as a 'snake' of a friend was something she didn't want to be reminded of everyday.

About midway through the third quarter, Mandi was called upon by her science teacher. His name was Gerald Blackwell. He was a tall black man in his 40s, who had a mustache and wore glasses. He had often observed Mandi since the beginning of the school year.

"Hi Mandi, could I speak with you for a minute?" he asked.

Mandi came over to him. "Yes," she said.

"I've watched you and have seen how well you've done in my class and… well, I was wondering, have you ever considered going off to college?"

Mandi smiled. "Yes. I would like to go to college," she answered.

"Have you thought of where you might want to go?"

Mandi shook her head. "Not really. I mean, I want to go, but I'm thinking of maybe working a job to pay my way through or help my mama."

Mr. Blackwell stared at her for a moment. "Well to me, you seem very smart and capable of going as far as you want to go in life. I truly mean that. You are a special child, one of my favorite students. So perhaps you might want to consider entering into an essay contest as to why you want to become a psychologist and the benefits a university will gain by selecting you for a scholarship."

Immediately, Mandi's eyes brightened like never before. Mr. Blackwell then pulled out an application that listed the requirements that a student had to fulfill to be considered for a full academic scholarship. Any student was eligible, but since Mandi had a history of good grades, her teacher considered her to be a high-level candidate to receive the award. The scholarship was limited to 30 African-American high school students who were female. So it was a fierce competition.

But to Mandi, she saw this as a golden opportunity of a lifetime and hugged her teacher, thanking him for thinking of her and most importantly, she assured him that she would win—and Mr. Blackwell believed it.

Mandi was so elated. After school, she went over to her mother's bakery shop and showed her the form. Thelma, whose hands were filled with flour, hugged Mandi, praying she would win. By the time she was done hugging her, the back of Mandi's clothes were covered in flour as well.

There was a deadline by which all essays had to be turned in, which was no later than the last day of June. Therefore, Mandi had plenty of time to prepare her thoughts in order to deliver the best essay she had ever written in her life. Mandi knew to follow the guidelines and instructions carefully so that she would be eligible. She knew that to be very important.

Secondly, she knew to add "winning the scholarship" to her dream book. Afterwards, she remained hopeful, looking at it everyday, believing that it would happen. There was really no worry or fear in Mandi of it not happening. She was more anxious about the thought of actually receiving it. She had not even decided what she would write about in the essay yet. All she knew and believed was that the universe would direct her.

So about a month before the school year ended, Mandi began to carefully compose her essay. It did take some time. Yet, she wasn't frustrated. Instead she remained calm, knowing that by writing just a few good sentences a day, she would eventually complete her paper to perfect form, which was how she treated it.

When she was finally done, she had her entire family read it, which had all of them in awe.

"You're gonna win, sis. I can feel it," said Darin.

"Yeah, this is good. You'll definitely win," smiled Carla.

"No question. You're gettin' that scholarship sistuh," added Rosaline.

Everyone was in full agreement and so encouraging that Mandi became excited by the thought.

Thelma hugged her tight. "I'm so proud of you baby!" she said, clutching her. "I know you'll win."

"Thanks mama," replied Mandi. "I already know too."

Thelma released Mandi and looked at her carefully, thrilled with what she saw. By this time, Mandi had grown to become such an attractive young lady. She was a mature woman so full of life, hope, promise and wonder combined, with a smile that could light up any room; a typical Godsend. Thelma was just short on words, unable to know what to say to her child, except to thank the good Lord for giving Mandi to her.

After a short pause, Thelma spoke. "Now let's go down to the post office together and help send this letter off in a parcel with my blessing."

"All right," Mandi smiled.

"Okay, let's go."

When they got to the post office, they delivered it with relief and the satisfaction that there was nothing left to do other than await her scholarship letter. After that, the two of them left together in smiles. Having her mother around always brought such confidence and joy to Mandi's soul. That same night, the two of them prayed over it, believing she'd be awarded the scholarship.

Six weeks went by quickly and it was early July. Mandi had come home early that afternoon from her mother's bakery. Soon, her brother Calvin appeared at the doorway holding her scholarship response letter. Carla and Rosaline were also beside him in excitement awaiting the results. Mandi immediately went over to grab the letter.

"Give it here," she said.

Calvin, wiggling it around, finally gave it to her.

"Naw, don't open it yet," suggested Rosaline suddenly. "Let's wait fo' mama and papa to come home. Then we'll read it."

Mandi, in spite of being excited, thought for a moment and agreed. "You know, we should," she said.

A few hours later, a tired Thelma along with Charlie arrived, not wanting to do anything except go to sleep. Darin also accompanied them.

"Mama, it came! It came! Look, here! It came!" shouted Mandi.

"What came?" Thelma wondered.

"My scholarship letter! It came! It came!" she exclaimed while shoving it in her face.

Thelma, now alert, became full of energy. "Well... what it say?" she asked.

"I don't know yet. We were waitin' fo' you and papa to show up."

"Well, what else ya waitin' on? You see we're here. Open it."

Mandi began to open it but the nervous tension inside her made her a bit hesitant and she asked her mother to open it.

"Now you know they got some big words in there that I can't read. Child, just open and read it. It ain't go'n hurt nuthin.'"

"Here I'll read it," offered Darin.

Mandi then brought the envelope back to herself away from Darin. "No, I'll read it," she said. "I wrote it, so *I* should know first what the letter says."

So gradually, Mandi began tearing through the flap while closing her eyes. Everyone was in such excitement and suspense.

"Will you just hurry up child... at least before this century runs out," hurried her father.

"Okay, okay," she responded. Mandi then took the letter from the envelope and with her eyes still closed, finally opened them to slowly read what was in the letter.

There was a moment of silence. "Okay, read on," demanded Thelma.

Rosaline suddenly tried sneaking behind her sister's shoulder.

"Girl move!" demanded Mandi, moving backwards.

Suddenly she began reading while everyone in front of her held their hands tight in anticipation.

Mandi read aloud: "*Dear candidate, Mandi Watkins. This letter is in response to your recent application for the college scholarship in social science. We are pleased to announce that you have just been selected for a full scholarship to...*"

Just then, everyone hugged her hard, nearly pushing her to the ground. She had won the scholarship and there was not one dry eye in sight.

7

Midwest Swing

MANDI WAS SO EXCITED ABOUT THE LETTER. AS SOON as her father heard the news, he couldn't help himself; he immediately grabbed the letter and jumped up and down like a child. He picked Mandi up in the air in absolute exhilaration. Thelma, who saw the whole scene, couldn't help but cry. Her baby was going off to college on a full scholarship.

"So what do you have to do now?" Thelma asked Mandi.

Mandi, who had not yet finished the entire letter, glanced over at it to read further. After finishing it, Mandi began to paraphrase.

"Uh, it says here that I should report to campus two weeks before the beginning of the fall quarter and give the letter to the bursar's office, where they will then keep it and make a record. Then, I will be assigned my room with a roommate. Failure to appear on that date may disqualify me from maintaining my scholarship."

"Well you bettuh keep the lettuh at a place where even God can't find it," Thelma said. "If you want, I'll hold onto it and put it in the safest place… "

"No mama, I got it," demanded Mandi.

"Well… is there anything else?" inquired Charlie.

Mandi looked at the letter again. "It says here that in order to maintain my scholarship, I have to have an 'A' average. Anything below that may cause me to lose it. I'm also required to complete fulltime credit hours during every quartuh, and not skip a quartuh. That seems to be pretty much it."

Mandi then folded the letter, placing it back in the envelope.

"Well, you bettuh do what they say and hold onto that lettuh. In fact, go put it somewhere safe now," Thelma commanded.

Mandi went on to do just that.

Thelma then went over to hug Charlie. "I can't believe it. Our baby's finally goin' off tuh college on a full scholah… I mean, scholuhship… after all she's been through," she cried. "I'm so *proud!*"

Charlie patted her on the back, smiling. "Yeah, I know," he said with his eyes watering. "I know. Me too."

Days later, Mandi went over to tell the rest of her siblings the good news. They were all happy for her. Francine, upon hearing the news, was equally ecstatic.

"I'm so proud of you, dear," she said. "What's the name of the school?"

"Uh, it's called Wayne College."

"Wow, never heard of it. Where's that at?"

"In… Detroit. Detroit, Michigan."

"So you got to go up north… to the Midwest then, right?"

Mandi nodded.

"Well congratulations. At least that'll allow you to have some exposure outside of this place. You'll be able to explore, expand your mind, and who knows… probably meet the love of your life."

Mandi smiled. "Like you said, 'who knows?'" she replied.

"So when're you going?"

"In about two weeks."

"Well that's great. How do you feel? Nervous?"

"A little, but I know I'm gonna be fine. I am going to miss you though."

"Well, it's not like you'll be gone forever. You can always write me and during holidays come visit me if you'd like."

"I'd like that very much."

"I heard though, it can get really chilly up there. So you might want to buy a coat. Up there is not like Mississippi. It's almost like being trapped in a freezer. It can *really* get cold."

"I know, I heard."

"You know, Mandi, I never went to college, so I don't know what it's like. But what I'm suggesting is that you do well there, you hear? I want you to just focus on your school work for the time being. Get good marks. Make me and your family proud, because I believe in you, child. You can do it. I know you can."

To hear that warmed Mandi's soul. That was all the encouragement she needed. This time, she went ahead and gave her mentor the biggest hug of her life. "I love you," she cried.

"I love you too child, but please be easy. You're hurting me. Remember, I'm not as young as I used to be."

"Yes ma'am."

"It's Francine. Just call me 'Francine.'"

"Yes Francine," Mandi replied, finally releasing herself from her.

The two of them chatted for several more minutes before Mandi decided to leave. It was getting dark. "Well I better get going," said Mandi.

"I think so too. Don't forget to call me once you arrive there. I just want to know how you're doing."

"I sure will Francine. Okay, bye now. Again, I love you."

"I love you too. Bye."

Mandi then waved back until she was finally out of Francine's sight.

Two weeks came, and Mandi flew with her parents to Detroit. Once they got there, they could easily feel a slight chill outside the airport, which gave them an instant reality check that they were no longer in the South. As soon as they left the airport, they boarded a cab, which took them to the school. On their way there, they marveled at the tall buildings and huge structures that existed in downtown Detroit. Many people crowded the streets, where there was the occasional honking of horns.

Both Charlie and Thelma, who had lived in Mississippi all their lives, instantly saw a whole new world. It appeared as if everyone was just on the go and in a hurry, where people tended to appear more laid back in Mississippi. Jackson was a decent metropolitan town, yet it appeared that Detroit had more activity.

As for Mandi, the entire scene was exciting. Every corner the cab turned led her to turn her head sideways, observing all that was in front of her. She saw the town as a means of exploration and exposure that she hardly could get back home. So she was even more grateful for the opportunity to attend. Detroit was now her playground.

When the family finally arrived at the campus, they got out of the car. Charlie paid the driver before he drove off. Once outside, the three of them stood in amazement and curiosity. Everything seemed beautiful and spacious. There were large fields and magnificent buildings. There were also a number of big libraries and major buildings within the campus, including sports arenas, science and art centers, along with areas of recreation. There were also a good number of students scattered throughout, walking in different directions.

After turning a few times, observing the scenery, Mandi pulled out the map of the campus from her side pocket, which she began to study, looking for the bursar's office. After figuring where they were on the map, she directed her parents where to go, and they proceeded. Once they got to the office, she filled out some paperwork, and was then directed to her boarding room across campus.

When she got there, she entered into her unit with a key, and met another young lady there.

"Hello, may I help you?" asked the young lady.

"Yeah, my name's Mandi. I'm assigned to live here."

"Oh really? Okay. Cool, cool. That's good. So am I. I live here too. My name's Calise."

"Looks like I'll be your roommate then."

"Yeah, I guess so."

The two of them shook hands. Calise was a black sophomore, age 21, whose major was sociology. She was wilder than she appeared. She liked to party and go out at night, hanging out with all her friends. However, she was still able to keep her schooling under control. She worked part time at night as a bartender, only to come home at 4 in the morning. When she wasn't bartending, she often listened to music or played the guitar. She smoked cigarettes, but had respect for people's space and privacy. Her motto was: "If you don't start anything, there won't be anything."

In all, she would be a person Mandi would get along with.

Mandi eventually brought her luggage to her room. Her room was quite simple. There was a bed, a dresser and a couch, which sat at the corner next to an end table. Suddenly, Mandi got all excited and jumped onto the bed face down. Charlie and Thelma just looked at each other smiling.

"So what'ch you gonna do now, baby?" Thelma asked.

"Sleep. I'm tired. Everything else, I'll figure out when I wake up."

"Well, me and yo' papa can help you while you sleep."

"But you don't know where anything goes."

"That's all right. We'll figure it out. I'm sure we won't be too far off."

Mandi, a little puzzled, suddenly became curious.

"Since when have you ever been so willin' to straighten my things out while I'm in the same room? And more importantly, why?"

There was no answer.

Mandi repeated the question, but still her mother didn't respond. Mandi then turned to her parents and instantly could see why. Her mother didn't want to leave her.

Mandi got up. "Mama," she said.

"Yes dear," Thelma answered, almost shaking.

By then, Thelma was in tears. Mandi went over to hug her mother tight, closing her eyes and Thelma wrapped her arms around her as well.

"Mama, don't cry. I'm gonna be fine. I promise."

"I know sweety. It's just that... I was so used to havin' you around, and I'm gone miss you. We all gone miss you."

"I'm gonna miss you too, but I promise, I'm gonna call you and papa as much as I can and come ovuh for Thanksgivin'. Okay?"

Thelma nodded wiping her tears. "Okay. Just make yo' mama and papa proud, okay? Can you do that fo' me?"

"Mama," Mandi said, looking squarely in her eyes. "That's all I know how to do."

Just then, Thelma smiled and hugged her daughter once again before kissing her.

"I know you will baby. I trust you."

Charlie went over to hug Mandi tight as well.

"I love you too, papa. Just make sho' you take care of mama, okay?"

"Now you know that that's all *I* know how to do… fo' almost 30 years now… and she aint left me yet. So what'ch you talkin' about?"

Mandi giggled.

"Oh and before I forget," said Thelma. "Here, I wanted you to have these… just in case. You nevuh know. So take it."

What she gave Mandi was a small brown paper bag. When Mandi opened it, she dipped her hand inside to see what it was, and low and behold, it was a roll of condoms.

"Mam*uuh*!" Mandi exclaimed. "I'm not doing anything."

"That's exactly why I'm givin' them to you…in case you do do something."

Mandi was embarrassed. Never in a million years did she imagine her mother would be that blunt, but Thelma continued on.

"Listen you nevuh know, now. I'm just trying to protect you from havin' babies so fast. That's all. Now I'm not sayin' you should go out there and do the 'do.' But if you *do*… at least you're covered. Now that's all I'm a say about that. I know we nevuh had that lil' *taulk* like mothuh and daughtuh, but I'm assumin' you already know the bidness and I jus' wanna make sho' you's safe. That's all."

"Mama, I don't need this."

"What, you got somethin' bettuh? You tryin' a tell me that a man won't look at you and not want what you got? Honey, let me tell you somethin'. In case you ain't figured out yet, I'm a woman, and women know women. And one thing I know is that most women are vuln'rable. Every man knows that all it takes is some sweet talk, some Marvin Gaye, mixed with some Al Green, o' Barry White, and a few *drinks*, and he's in there. It happens *every* time. By the time you even get to yo' senses to know what's goin' on, it's been too late already… jus' like that," she said snapping her fingers. "And sometimes… he aint even got to do all that wining and dining. I mean… 'cause it's already *there*… waitin'."

Both Mandi and her father couldn't help but laugh out loud.

"Hey, I'm only bein' real," added Thelma. "Truth *is* what it is... 'cause that's *all* it is!"

Charlie just could not help laughing since he wanted to pretend like he didn't hear anything. To him, this was a female matter and he wanted nothing to do with it whatsoever. But he knew Thelma was right, judging from their experience together.

"Listen, you just hold on to it, ya hear?" Thelma said. "Who knows, you may nevuh have to use it. I'm just helping ya be careful. That's all. If you don't ever use'em, you can always throw'em away. But...just not now."

Mandi was short of words, but could easily see her point, and therefore said nothing.

"Well it looks like me and yo' papa gone head out. We wanna have enough time befo' we catch our flight back."

"Okay."

"Now don't forget to call us now... makin' sho e'rything's all right, ya hear? If there's evuh a problem, you call us. I hope you still got the numbuh. Just remembuh when you call, to dial one, then the area code, because since you're outta state and... "

"Mama I got it. Trust me. I'll call."

There was a moment of silence.

"She's got it baby. Just relax. She'll be all right," added Charlie.

Thelma then looked at Mandi once more and smiled.

"I love you baby. You take care now, okay? You're all grown up now. And don't forget to make us proud. It's a Watkins tradition... at least it supposed to be, anyway."

Mandi smiled and walked back out with her parents. Before they went out completely, they waved to Calise who waved back. Soon after, Mandi and her parents exchanged a few more words before finally hugging one last time, waving and blowing kisses.

As soon as Mandi shut the door, she leaned her back against it, blowing a full breath of hot air with her arms crossed.

"Detroit, here I am," she said.

And indeed, she was. It was now her world.

8

A Sticky
Situation

THREE YEARS HAD PASSED AND NOW MANDI WAS IN HER senior year at college during the fall quarter. She couldn't wait to graduate. Just the thought of it gave her a tickling sensation. She would be the second in her family to graduate, followed by her brother Jimmy who was the first. All she could think about was the reaction of her parents once they saw their daughter walk on stage.

She could think of it for hours. And the more she thought of it, the more she smiled just believing that it was already present. From there, the thought of her party and all her friends who would be there was all so much fun to dream about. By then, she had become so obsessed about graduating, that she thought about doubling her class load so as to finish faster. But she eventually thought that it wasn't wise and decided to just take the regular course load until she finished.

On one afternoon, Mandi sat inside a study hall highlighting some sentences from her textbook. After about an hour, she felt a little exhausted and decided to take a break and walk around the building. So she marked her page, closed the book, left the hall, and went to the student center. Mandi began walking around for several minutes before finding a juice machine located next to a staircase and bathroom.

Mandi glanced at the machine and searched in her pocket for any loose change, which she had. From her pocket came four quarters, which was enough to select the juice of her choice. She particularly loved pineapple juice and selected just that. When the bottle finally fell down the slot, Mandi reached down, grabbed it, and walked away.

Yet, for some reason, she was in the mood for a little more exercise and decided to go through the doorway beside the juice machine and go up the staircase to the third floor.

When she entered the staircase, she noticed some repair work being done, and the mild scent of paint, although all the walls were dry. There were also a few layers of wood and some minor debris near the walls. When she looked behind her, she saw that the frame of the doorway she went through was almost near completion.

After glancing at everything, she walked a few more steps and noticed a colorful flyer inviting students to attend a local dance party that was coming up. Mandi read it while opening her bottle. Several seconds later, she proceeded to walk away, simultaneously bumping into a young man.

"Excuse me," said the man, coming from the men's room.

Mandi had bumped into him full force, causing her to lose full control of her bottle, spilling her pineapple juice on his shirt before dropping it to the ground where it splashed on his boots. There was a puddle of the juice still left on the floor and the bottle was empty. Mandi was in complete shock and felt embarrassed.

"Oh, my God. I am so *so* sorry. It was an accident. I didn't know. It's all my fault," she said.

The poor guy just looked at her smiling. "Listen please, wait right there. Hold on. Let me get something," she said.

Just then, she rushed over to the woman's bathroom and collected a lot of paper towels, blotted them with water, and added soap. After that, she immediately attended to the guy who was still standing there, waiting.

Without hesitation, Mandi began softly rubbing the wet paper towel on the juice stain on his shirt, which was wet. After she was done with his shirt, she bent down to wipe any juice from his boots, which wasn't much. Then she cleaned the puddle on the floor. She grabbed the empty bottle and proceeded back to the women's bathroom to throw everything away and get more paper towels, sure to remove any last stickiness from the floor.

As soon as she was done, the man just stood there, staring at her with admiration. Again, Mandi tried apologizing; but the quiet man finally broke his silence.

"Listen, I heard you the first time. You don't have to keep apologizing. You did the best job any woman could do. I like that."

Mandi gave a crooked smile, looking a bit at his chest but no further. "Au thank you," she said. "I just hope it's not too bad. Hopefully it doesn't get sticky on you."

"No it's fine. Believe me, I'll live," said the man. "Hey why don't you look at me? I hope I'm not *that* ugly."

"No, no. You're fine. It's just that… I… I just can't believe I did this."

"So you still feel embarrassed?"

Mandi nodded, looking down to the floor with her right hand over her forehead.

"Well… if you feel that bad about it, why don't you make it up by having dinner with me some time this week?"

At that point, Mandi instantly looked straight at him. "I beg your pardon," she said.

"You don't have to beg nothin'. You *heard* me. Have dinner with me this week. And don't worry, I'll pay. By then, all this… *thing* you're feeling, can all go away."

"You're serious?" she replied.

"Look, one thing you'll know about me is that I don't lie."

Mandi was short of words, smiling. That was always good to hear. "But… but why?" she asked.

"Well for one, I liked how you handled this. That shows good character. You're a girl who cares. And secondly… you just seem like a very special kind of woman. Since you're a student, my guess is you're very smart, probably fun, and disciplined. Plus, I love your accent. And to top it all off, you're a *sistah* with all these qualities that not too many women I know have. I also like your smile and I think you're very gorgeous and attractive, especially when you act shy. In fact, I think you're the most gorgeous when you're shy."

Right then, Mandi could not resist but put on a bigger smile. In her mind, she trusted that this was the universe working in full affect.

"So what do ya say? Dinner?" he asked.

Just then another man stuck his head through the door frame, looking at him.

"Is everything okay? Are we done yet?" asked the man peaking through.

"Yeah Marcus, I just have to screw this frame back together, then we'll be all set. I'll be done in a minute. It's just that this fine young lady wants to give me her number so I can take her out," he said smiling.

Just then, Marcus laughed before stepping back outside the frame. "Okay. Well in that case, carry on. We'll be outside, waiting," he said before finally leaving.

Mandi couldn't help but laugh, and playfully tapped the guy on his chest.

"How dare you put me on the spot like that. I never said that," she said.

"I know, but you were about to. Weren't you? And besides, relax, he's just a co-worker. We're contracted to do some repairs on the ceilings and walls and doors. The school wanted most of this place to be remodeled. That's why we're here."

"So you do home repairs?" Mandi asked.

"Yup, pretty much. You can pretty much call me a handy man."

There was then a small pause between the two of them as Mandi began turning her head around noticing all the new improvements.

"So what's you're name?" the man asked.

"Oh... uh, Mandi."

"Mandi? That's a nice name. I'm Ronnie," he said, extending his hand to greet. "Pleased to meet you."

"Pleased to meet you too, Ronnie," she replied, shaking his hand.

"So... help me out. You pick the place and time and I'll be right there."

"Oh... okay, if you insist. How 'bout we meet across the street at Ruger's Square on Thursday. I'm free Thursday. Are you?"

"Mmm.... yeah. What time you wanna meet?"

"Mmm... is seven good?"

"Yeah. Seven's good. By then, all the stains will have disappeared," he joked. "And I won't be late. So don't worry."

"Good. I hope not. So you got the date down? You know the place? The time? The day?"

"It's all in here," he said pointing to his head.

"Okay, see ya then."

"See ya. Again it was a pleasure meeting you Mandi," he said suddenly grabbing her right hand and blessing it with a kiss.

That gesture made Mandi's body tingle. It was an exciting feeling. It was clear. Ronnie was a gentleman.

"Na... nice to meet you too," she replied, feeling a bit shaky.

After a few moments, the two parted ways, yet Mandi turned her head one more time to glance at him before waving excitedly, going up the stairs. By the time she got back to her chair where she left all her materials, she found it difficult to study. The thought of Ronnie and just his bold move toward her seemed all too sudden and unreal. How she was able to agree to a date that quickly was beyond her comprehension. It was almost like she didn't even know when she accepted it.

But in actuality, she honestly believed that it was the universe sending her a signal of a soul mate, which she wanted... bad. And with the fact that he wasn't at all bad looking either, this just had to work out, so she thought. Therefore, her spilling the bottle on him was no accident. It was all by design. Just as Francine had told her always, claiming that with the law of attraction, there were no mistakes. Everything was divinely set in place to cause an occurrence through the messages it receives from one's own mind.

And as Francine also said, such occurrences will come when one least expects it; similar to when she met her husband John. And as designed, Mandi had no idea or expectation that such an event would bring this result that quickly. However, having a mate was truly one of her goals.

On Thursday, Mandi chose to wear a black dress where the skirt end felt as soft as a feather, just gliding in whichever direction she turned. Along with that she put on make up and special perfume. Plus, she took good care of her hair. She was absolutely beautiful. And at 5'5 and 128 pounds with a breast size of 32C, what wasn't there to like? So while still in her room, she glanced in her mirror once more, feeling excited, before heading out to *Ruger's Square*.

Ten minutes to 7 p.m., Ronnie stood there waiting for her. He was sharp, which put an instant smile on Mandi's face. He had on a dress jacket and dress shirt with tightly pressed khaki pants and dress shoes. He was dressed for the occasion. He also had sharp sporting waves showing on the front of his head, which was also impressive.

"It's so nice to meet you again," he said. "You look *wonderful.*"

"Thank you. You look good too."

"Thanks. I found a table where we can sit and look at a menu. Sound good?"

"Okay."

Ronnie directed her to a side corner of the restaurant where the two later sat and opened their menus. From there, their conversation continued.

Ronnie was an interesting man. He was 25. Since he was 12, he always liked to do things with his hands. His father owned a mechanic's shop where Ronnie learned to work on cars. Along with that, Ronnie took on a job working for his uncle, doing landscaping during the summer and home repair work during the winter. So he stayed busy all year round. The concept of school didn't really appeal to him. He dropped out at age 16, deciding to work for his uncle until maybe he could own his own business. However, Ronnie knew how to read and write proficiently.

As time went by, he did other things to make some money. He was just a natural-born hustler, plain and simple. Apart from working with his dad at times on cars, he would shine shoes for people in the neighborhood. At age 19, he and another guy established a residential carpet cleaning business, which made good money. But based on the fact that he was in so many other kinds of trades, helping people in other areas, that didn't last too long. Working for people became his passion. He was a constant workaholic, always looking for something to do.

He was rarely in a steady relationship because he was just too busy. He had a gift in repairing nearly any part of a home. He could do roofing, windows, plumbing, flooring, walls and doors. He could remodel an entire room. The only thing that he couldn't do too well was electrical work. He could change a wall socket, but any major repair, such as re-wiring a whole house, required a real expert in that field, and he wasn't one of them. Thoughts of one of his close friends getting electrocuted to death while doing wiring gave Ronnie a phobia of fully engaging in that line of work. So he left it alone.

Even though he was a workaholic, he also knew how to have fun. He would sometimes go to parties and flirt with the ladies. He loved football, especially college. He was a huge Wolverine fan. Saturdays were usually a full workday for him, but he always made an effort to go to at least two of their games during the season. He dreamed of going to one of their games against Ohio State, but the tickets were always too expensive. Yet all the same, he was an all-around fun guy, always interested in making people happy and trying to deliver fair work as best as he could. But the company he now worked for was a corporate entity that had contracts with certain schools for repairs.

Mandi enjoyed the conversation. Ronnie was funny and had a smooth demeanor. He was honest and wasn't uptight. He always looked at Mandi whenever he spoke and would patiently listen to her speak, which always exceeded more than he was able to talk. Their date lasted for roughly two hours, from which of course, he paid the bill as promised.

"So I guess I paid you with my time for what I did to your shirt, right?" Mandi asked.

"Yeah… something like that."

"So I guess I won't be seeing you again."

"I don't know. Would you want to?"

Mandi smiled. "Mmm… *maybe*," she replied.

"Maybe? What do you mean, 'maybe'? 'Cause I definitely want to see you again. I want to see a lot more of you... if I could."

Mandi then reached for her black purse and removed a piece of paper, which had a home phone number already written down, and above it, her class schedule.

"I don't work. So you can find me either at the school or call me," she said.

Ronnie looked at it. "Excellent," he said. "Let me give you my number. If I don't answer, I'm probably at a job somewhere, but I'll definitely call back when I get a chance."

"Sounds good," she said.

Just then, the two of them rose from the table and left the restaurant. They took a short walk around the block together. Mandi looked up in the sky and noticed the full moon glimmering with brightness. It was beautiful, shining brighter than she could ever remember. She smiled, wondering if that was a sign that she had found her man.

"You know Mandi, I want to tell you something if you don't mind," Ronnie began.

"Sure say it," she said.

Before he could, they stopped at a halt and stood together beside a parking lot; Ronnie looked in her eyes.

"Do you believe in fate?" he asked.

"I do."

"Do you think fate brought us together?"

"Well, I'm not... sure. It probably did. Why?"

"Because our meeting in that hallway gave me some kind of feeling that it wasn't by accident that you spilled that juice on me. I just think that nature wouldn't have had it any other way than for that to occur so we would be standing right here at this moment. Seriously, I have never asked a girl out like I did with you before. It may appear that way but I haven't, I swear... but something made me just approach you that way and speak out when I had no idea what I was even saying.

Honestly. I think about it, and say, 'Man. I said all that?' And wouldn't you believe that I was just wrapping up with about 15 minutes left to go and then I'd be done with the job, and then you showed up. Seriously, the crew was just waiting for me to finish. We were already done. All that was left was just measuring and putting a few screws together. So… so… I don't know, but that's why I asked if you believe in fate."

Mandi just smiled in amazement while he spoke, looking up at the moon. She had finally got her answer. Right then, she took one step forward to him.

"You know, there's no need figuring it out. All that matters is that we're here now, in the moment. All we have to do is just take it one step at a time and see where it leads us. But I definitely want to see you again because I do love this moment and what I'm feeling right now. Honestly, I've never felt this way before. So I'm interested in seeing what will happen."

Soon after, Mandi stretched her arms out and hugged him gently as he did the same, which lasted more than a few seconds.

"See me as often as you'd like," she said. "I would like that very much."

"I will," he promised.

When they finished hugging, he asked: "Do you need a ride home?"

"No. I don't live far at all," she said.

"Well okay. You take care, okay?"

"You do the same," she smiled.

Before they finally parted, Ronnie went over and gave Mandi a quick kiss on the cheek, which dazzled her. Then he left and went to his car, which was very loud, almost as if there was a hole in the muffler. However, Mandi paid no attention to it. She was oblivious to what was going on, thinking only of what had just happened, almost without even realizing he had taken off. She just hoped this intense feeling wouldn't distract her from her studies. As soon as she was finally in touch with reality again, she raced home, excited, as if she had just won the Michigan Lottery.

9

Phone
Call

A FEW MONTHS HAD PAST AND MANDI WAS IN HER LAST quarter of school. She had only three more classes left before she would get her degree. She was so excited. Finally, she was going to be the first daughter to finish college. Upon hearing the good news, her mother couldn't have been happier. She was so proud that she was almost in tears, realizing how an event like this would have never come about had it not been for Francine. Thelma and Charlie would express just complete joy hearing of their daughter's progress. In fact, all Mandi's siblings were proud of her and wished her the best. And that was all the encouragement Mandi needed. Everything just felt so good.

During the quarter, Mandi wrote to her parents about Ronnie, telling them how good of a man he was. They would see each other twice each week, which was understandable, since Ronnie was always on a job and Mandi needed to focus on school. They were both chasing success through their own respective paths. Though it was clear, the bond they shared was more than just friendship. In fact, Mandi had already told Ronnie that she loved him, and he responded accordingly.

Mandi knew her parents would want to meet him, especially her mother, who would instinctively ask out loud when they were getting married. Therefore, Mandi wanted to hold off introducing Ronnie to them until marriage was definite. Mandi didn't want Ronnie or herself to be embarrassed with the questions Thelma would start asking. But in Mandi's mind, if asked, she would say "yes." In fact, she was hoping Ronnie would propose right after she graduated. She would view it as the best graduation present ever. However as much as Mandi anticipated, Ronnie never brought up the subject.

The final quarter went by fast, and Mandi prepared her cap and gown for commencement. Her parents were so excited and they flew out for the ceremony. They could hardly contain themselves. When they arrived, they each went over to hug Mandi, who was near a conference hall along with the other students, waiting for the ceremony to start.

"You look good baby. *Now*, where's that man you keep tellin' me about?" Thelma asked suddenly while searching around.

"Oh… uh… he's right here," Mandi replied.

Right behind Thelma stood Ronnie, who came around to shake her hand.

"What'ch ya doin' son?" Thelma asked Ronnie strangely. "We're from the South and in the South, we don't shake hands. We give hugs, okay? So c'mon, get it right. Come give me a big hug. You never know, I just might be your mother-in-law some day. So you gotta treat me right now, ya hear? Mandi already told me *so* much about you."

"Mama, please. Stop."

"*What?* Ya'll done been together already fo' this long. You might as well get married. Ya'll done seen pretty much everything ya'll need to see, so why not go 'head get it over wit'? And he's handsome too. Child, what you wastin' time fo'?"

Ronnie along with everyone started laughing.

"Mama, please. Not now. Later."

"What? Ya'll ain't getting' no younger. Ya'll need to hurry up and quit wastin' time. At least do it some time before I leave this earth... "

"Mama, please!" Mandi pleaded desperately.

Thelma stopped and turned to Ronnie, whispering. "You go 'head marry my daughter, ya hear? She won't let ya down. I promise."

She then winked at him before turning to her daughter. "I'm just sayin'," she told Mandi. "It is what it is."

Ronnie just laughed while Mandi covered her face in shame. Though part of it was funny, she hoped her mother hadn't embarrassed Ronnie too much. Yet at the same time, Mandi was glad Ronnie was getting the signal, since that was exactly what she wanted. So it was a good and a bad thing that Thelma opened her mouth the way she did.

Ronnie then approached Mandi, smiling. "You know, I like your mom already. She's all right."

Mandi was stunned. "Really?" she wondered.

"Yeah. She doesn't shy away from anything. She just keeps it real. And I like that."

Mandi could not believe her ears, but smiled with joy. "Oh... well thanks," she smiled. "That's mama. What you see is what you get."

There was then a slight pause. "Then maybe we *should* get married after all," she joked, bravely. "Yuh know, I'm just sayin'."

Ronnie just smiled.

About an hour after the ceremony commenced, Mandi finally walked on stage, shaking hands with the university president as her family along with Ronnie roared for her achievement. Thelma suddenly broke down in tears. Later on, after the ceremony, there was of course the taking of pictures of Mandi and her family and of course, Ronnie. Afterwards, the family went to a local restaurant to celebrate. When they got there, they sat at a long table. Ronnie sat next to Mandi, while the rest of the family sat around them. Everyone had a nice time. By the time it was over, everyone hugged Mandi before going back to Mississippi. It was a moment that neither Mandi nor the family would ever forget.

A few months passed and Mandi began searching for a job. She was considering working with children who were victims of abuse. However, she didn't feel pressured, since she knew that a certain guide would lead her to the right calling.

That evening, Ronnie came over to visit. He still had his own place and she had hers. When he got there, they embraced and kissed while in the living room.

"So how was work?" Mandi asked.

"Well, you know. Same old, same old."

Mandi nodded her head, showing a slight grin as if she wanted to say something but was hesitant. Yet her expression showed a bit of frustration, which Ronnie could easily sense from their time together.

"Ronnie, what's going on?" she blurted out suddenly.

"Whoa!… what do you mean? Nothing's going on."

"That's exactly right. *Nothing* is going on."

Ronnie, a little confused, was desperate for an explanation. "Okay. Tell me, what is it I did this time?"

Mandi shook her head. "It's not what you did that's the problem. It's what you haven't done."

"Like what?"

"How come you haven't proposed to me yet? I mean, it has been over a year since we've gone out and three months since I've graduated and I was hoping that you would have asked me by now. I mean must I spell it out? You know I didn't want to embarrass you on that day my mom came, but she *is* right, you know. We either get it done or not do it at all."

"Listen I'm not ready yet."

"Then when will you be ready Ronnie? Tell me, what is that *thing* that's holding you back from just making a decision? Are you scared? Is it other girls, or my education, or did you just think that this shackin' up was going to be forever? Because if so, this shackin' up has now just came with a price. It's no longer free. You have to put a commitment behind it this time."

"Wait, what do mean it's no longer free? I thought I have been paying for it, through taking you out, buying you stuff, and besides, you already know I'm trying to get some funds straightened out."

"Funds, funds, funds. That's all I ever hear from you. Listen, don't worry about that right now. Though it's important, if you just make the commitment, everything else will take care of itself."

"How?"

"That's just it. The 'how' is not important. All I can say is that the universe will create instances in our life to make us have a good wedding. But I want it to come from your heart. I really don't want to force it on you, because then, it won't work. But please be honest with me. Don't waste my time. I'm 22 and even my youngest sister, Rosaline, is married."

"So is that what this is about? Competition? Marriage is not something you just rush… "

"Make a decision Ronnie!" she yelled. "That's all I'm telling you."

For a moment there was silence between them. Then Ronnie looked at her closely, recognizing her tone of voice.

"Aw… are you on your period?" he asked.

"Yeah. How ya figure?"

"A… a lot of ways."

At this moment, Ronnie could sense he was in trouble. However at that same instant, the phone rang. Mandi stood still and stared at Ronnie strangely, pretending not to hear it. Whenever she did that, Ronnie could always sense it was better he just left the scene entirely. Though this time, he was saved by the bell—the phone bell.

"The phone's ringing," he said.

"I know. I'll get it."

She went over and grabbed the phone. "Yes, hello," she said.

It was a call from Thelma. Apparently Francine had fallen ill and told Thelma about it. Thelma was not comfortable with just knowing. She wanted to let Mandi know so that she could come back home and visit Francine. In fact, it wasn't even an option. Thelma insisted that Mandi go and see her mentor and savior.

When Mandi heard this, she felt distraught. Just the other day, Francine gave her $500 as a graduation gift, and now she was sick. What was amazing was that Francine never appeared as anyone who would ever get sick. Though she was 67, she was still so full of life and energy. So after hearing this, Mandi made it her duty to go and see her and promised Thelma that she would call her when she arranged for travel. Afterwards, Mandi then slammed down the phone.

"What is it?" Ronnie asked.

"It's a dear friend of mine. Her name's Francine. I've known her since I was 12. She's sick."

"Why what's the problem?"

"She has leukemia. And my mom suggested I go visit her."

"Are you?"

"Of course."

"Where?"

"Down south Mississippi."

"Well good luck. When you going?"

"Next week."

A short pause came between them again. Then Mandi thought of an idea. "Listen. How 'bout you come with me? It'll just be for about three days and then we'll come back. Just think of it as our little vacation together, just you and me. C'mon, *please.*"

"That's all good, but why me?"

"Because… I just want you with me and I desperately want you to meet this woman. She's real inspirational and was the one who saved my life. I'm sure when you see her, you'll like her. I promise you. *And* she has a big house too. At least do it for me. *Please.*"

Suddenly she approached him, kissing his cheek and neck, uttering the word "please" as she reached under his shirt to rub his belly button.

"Well… if… if it means that much to you… I'll… I'll go," he succumbed.

Mandi jumped up and down in excitement, hugging him. "Thank you. Thank you, so much. I promise you won't regret it."

"Can I get some now?" asked Ronnie.

Mandi thought for a minute. "*Boy*, I'm on my period. Remember? And besides you still have a commitment to make first. So… the answer is, 'no, you *ain't* gettin' it.' As soon as you make a commitment, *then* I just might give you the master key."

They both laughed. Mandi couldn't even believe that those words came out of her mouth. But of course, things were much easier said then done.

The following week, the two of them arrived at the airport in Jackson to be greeted by Mandi's family. There, the two of them met Thelma, Charlie and Rosaline, who was carrying her six-month-old son. They then entered Charlie's car where they went to the house as the couple's resting ground.

Since they had only three days, Mandi and Ronnie made sure to relax for the evening in order to see Francine the following day, which was exactly what happened.

The following morning Mandi and Ronnie got dressed to go out to visit. Since Francine's home was in the suburban area, they decided to call a cab to take them there. And since there was no telling how long the two of them would be there, they found no reason to have Charlie drop them off and then wait for them. Besides, they were adults. Mandi also wanted to use the time to spend personally with Francine. She didn't want any of her family involved. To her, this was a private matter.

When they arrived, Ronnie paid the cab driver and the two of them got out of the car. What he saw in front of him was beyond wonder: a magnificent villa. The property still looked just as Mandi remembered from years ago, except for a few add-ons here and there.

There were still the rose bushes that bordered the middle entrance way leading to the estate. The entire yard was in impeccable shape. The grass, which was freshly cut, hadn't one crab grass in sight. There were flowers throughout, with workers watering parts of the grass, while doing other chores. The mansion itself was a sight to see. It had about six separate balconies just on the front and sides of the house. God only knew what lay inside.

"Wow," Ronnie stared in amazement. "I tell ya, if I ever had to do any work in this place, I'd add an extra zero to what I normally charge people."

Mandi smiled. "See. I told you you'd like it. But you ain't seen nothin' yet. C'mon."

As soon as they arrived, they rang the bell next to the doorway that was as tall as Mandi and Ronnie put together.

Suddenly, a maid opened the door. "May I help you?" she asked.

"Yes. We're here to see Francine. She's expecting us," Mandi said.

The maid stared at Ronnie and Mandi up and down before telling them to wait. After a few minutes, she returned.

"I'm afraid she's sleeping at the moment. Do you mind coming back another time?"

"Well actually we do," Mandi replied. "See, we're coming from Detroit and want to visit her since we heard she's sick."

"Again, who are you?"

"Mandi. My mama, Thelma, worked for her here for 30 years."

The maid glanced at them again. "Well I'm afraid she's sleeping. Come back another time."

"But we're not coming back," Mandi stated, getting louder. She then took a deep breath, before continuing. "Ma'am listen, I'm not trying to cause any trouble here. I'm really not. But it's obvious you see two black people standing here and suddenly believe we don't belong anywhere on this property, but this woman is the reason I'm alive today talking to you, which is why I can never live with myself if I don't see her again, since this may be my last opportunity we may ever see face to face. So please, I beg of you, remove the color stigma and kindly wake her up and tell her that Mandi Watkins is here to see her. That's all I ask. Again, I don't mean any harm or disrespect, but this is really, really important to me. I need to see her."

Surprised by Mandi's remark, the maid asked them to wait another minute. Minutes later the maid returned.

"Come on in," she said.

As they entered, the two of them witnessed a palace. "Please follow me," the maid said.

The couple did, and they were soon welcomed in a room where Francine was sitting in a wheelchair. As soon as Mandi saw her, she went over to hug her dear friend. Francine then smiled. "Oh... how are you my child?"

"Great. I'm still trying to remain positive."

"That's good and who's this fine young man you got here? Is he your husband?"

"Uh... no. He... "

"Oh, well don't worry about it. He will be soon. I already can feel it. I can tell a husband when I see one. Come here young man, give me a hug. I always like hugs."

Ronnie went over and hugged her gently.

"That's a good lad," Francine said tapping his back.

Just then, the maid entered the room with a tray of fruits, sandwiches, bread and crackers, which delighted Ronnie and Mandi so much that they couldn't wait to dig in.

"Please help yourselves. We've got some time," encouraged Francine.

Mandi and Ronnie began snacking on the food. As they ate, Mandi began to ask Francine about her disease. Francine expressed much hope and optimism that she would be cured. She couldn't explain it, but believed she would be fine. She only mentioned the condition to Thelma so that she was aware. Though Francine didn't partake in any drugs or surgery. She just continued to eat raw fruits and vegetables, exercise, smile, and practice positive thinking.

During their time together, Francine began to learn about Ronnie and the rest of Mandi's family. The three of them laughed and had a joyous time. A couple hours passed and the couple was eventually told that Francine was expecting other guests. But before they would leave, Francine called Ronnie to come to her.

Since Francine could not stand well, Ronnie came and kneeled down before her so that Francine could hold his head while talking to him, looking straight in his eyes.

"Now listen to me, Ronnie," Francine said. "I am an excellent judge of character and through our brief moments together, I can sense already you're a good man. Even though I may not know all there is about you, I already know you're a good man. And any good man needs a good woman. That woman you got right there, called Mandi, is a good woman. Believe me, I know. Her spirit, her energy and drive are more valuable and sacred than all the precious jewelry I hold dear in my chest drawer upstairs. You have a gem, an ace. She's never told me to say any of this. I'm just speaking from the heart. I've known her since she was 12 and I've watched her grow and if you come across anyone that knows me, they will tell you that I don't lie or mislead anyone for the sake of someone else. I don't play games. I tell it as it is. Now… you can decide not to take my advice and go elsewhere and chase other diamonds you feel are out there, but a true diamond is really hard to find, especially when it's scattered among cubic zirconias, *if* you know what I mean. It becomes harder to tell the difference each time you pick one up. Understand me?"

"Yes ma'am."

"Just call me *Francine.*"

"Yes Francine."

"Good. What you got there is a real precious jewel. So don't lose her, because people like her don't come easy. They're very rare. The greatest drillers in the world still search for oil and precious minerals, because they're rare in nature and don't come easy. But as for you, you can stop digging because she's right there. So you think about that and count your blessings for the woman you have."

Ronnie suddenly had a big smile on his face. "Thank you Francine."

"Thank *you* for listening. Now you be good, okay? And take care of her. She's yours."

"I will."

"Good man. Now, if you all will excuse me, I do have other company and business to attend to. Yet it was a pleasure you all could come down and see me."

Mandi, whose heart was melting the entire time Ronnie heard that speech, thanked Francine for her time as did Ronnie. It wasn't long before the maid was called to escort them out. As they were guided through the hallway, the maid, who was leading them, was immediately called upon for an errand, which caused her to abandon them temporarily.

"Excuse me for a moment," she said to them. "But I'll be right back... or... or perhaps you both can let yourselves out?"

Both Mandi and Ronnie nodded. "We know the way," said Mandi. Mandi still remembered parts of the home as a result of her constant visits during her childhood.

At that moment, the maid left, leaving Ronnie and Mandi all by themselves. Mandi suddenly began to proceed to the direction of the exit until an emotional Ronnie quickly grabbed her hand, pulling her back to him, looking at her with excitement.

"Listen baby," he said. "Sorry I've been so stubborn lately. But the feeling I felt in that room with that woman was so amazing, I couldn't believe it. You *have* been all I've been looking for, for a long time. And even though I may not understand it, I *do* feel it and I trust it. And I know we may have a lot of things to sort out, but I'd rather sort them out tomorrow than not have you with me today. So what I'm asking you now is: Mandi Elizabeth Watkins, will you marry me?"

Mandi looked at him in shock, expressing an emotion of someone about to cry. Her eyes instantly watered. Not only had she never heard Ronnie ever talk that way before, but those were the sweetest words she had ever heard in her life, even if it was a question. Also he remembered her middle name.

"Aw Ronnie," she said, drying her eyes. "I thought you'd never ask."

There was then a pause. Then, after a brief moment, Ronnie became anxious. She still hadn't answered him.

"Well... " he wondered impatiently.

Mandi then caught herself. "Oh… uh sorry," she said. "I mean: *Yes! Yes! I will!*"

Immediately, Ronnie held her in the air whirling her around before kissing her ferociously as if they were in a hotel room. While this was happening, Mandi instantly thought for a moment, suggesting Ronnie calm down.

"Listen, why don't we celebrate at a hotel? You can do whatever you want with me there. You have the master key!"

Suddenly, Ronnie's eyes opened up like saucers. "Oh… then let's go," he said.

After saying that, Ronnie caught Mandi off guard, instantly grabbing her by the arm toward the entranceway of Francine's home, where they left and rushed for a taxi. Once the taxi arrived, it took them to the closest hotel possible. As soon as they got there, Ronnie paid the driver plus a nice tip. They then got to their room where Ronnie was sure to deliver what they both wanted so desperately!

10

Mrs. Harris

MANDI WAS SO EXCITED THAT SHE WAS FINALLY getting married. As soon as she and Ronnie returned from their hotel stay, she told her parents the good news before they even had a chance to welcome her back. Thelma of course hugged Ronnie hard, saying, "Welcome to the family, son." Charlie also commended him. Then suddenly Thelma began interrogating him about his faith, his own family, where the wedding would be held, and many other questions about the upcoming event.

Of course nothing had been decided yet, since the news was only hours old. So as civilized people, Mandi and Ronnie agreed that they would return home and plan everything, and *then* call her family with the details. Though, of course, the wedding was going to be held in Mississippi.

The following day, the two of them returned to Detroit. As with most newly engaged women, so many thoughts began racing through Mandi's mind about the future. Mandi wanted to have at least three children, at least one boy and one girl, so she could have a taste of both worlds. She just wasn't too keen on having as large of a family as her parents did. Without even having kids yet, she sensed that the waiting time along with the labor was just no fun at all. Like her mother, Mandi loved the pleasure a great deal. She just didn't want to have to pay for it every time.

Of course, she and Ronnie had sex… a lot. And to her, Ronnie was a good lover. He was "Mr. Fix It," which was why she carried protection, always. It was almost like Thelma was a psychic because the type of protection that she gave Mandi years earlier was very similar to what she began using.

Ronnie eventually took Mandi to visit her future father-in-law, Willie Harris. He and Mandi had met a few times prior, but since this occasion was a special one, he made sure to make time and introduce her to his two brothers and older sister who were waiting to welcome Mandi when she arrived.

Ronnie's mother, Dianne, died of heart failure when Ronnie was a child, leaving behind three girls and a boy. As for Ronnie's sisters, Mandi would eventually meet them within the upcoming months as well. Mandi was happy to meet all of Ronnie's family members, since it confirmed that the plan of marriage was definite.

To have a wedding required money, and Mandi knew that. So she went and got a job as a cashier at a local supermarket. It was a bit odd since she already had a degree. However, she saw it as the quickest way to earn money for the wedding before eventually taking her time to carefully choose a job in her field.

The date was not yet set, but the couple decided to save as much as they could before beginning to plan the event. Charlie and Thelma agreed to help out as well. Willie, Ronnie's father, was going to do the same. Since Ronnie was his only son, he wanted to make sure that he was taken care of. Since the wedding was going to be held down South, both Ronnie and Mandi were in constant communication with Thelma and Charlie as far as the location of the wedding and other details. During this time, Ronnie and Mandi sent money to Mandi's parents to arrange everything. A week before the wedding, Ronnie and Mandi would arrive in order to prepare themselves for what would unfold before them.

Four months later, Mandi and Ronnie were able to send Charlie and Thelma $3,250 for the wedding. With the exception of Mandi's dress, the wedding attire was bought and tailored accordingly. Mandi's brother, Darin, would be Ronnie's best man. Mandi had selected Carla as her maid of honor, and her other four sisters to be bridesmaids; married or not, she wanted her family by her side that day.

Upon her arrival, Mandi received the wedding dress her mother wore to her wedding with Charlie. It was simple yet rich in history, having been in the family for three generations, starting with Thelma's mother, who wore it first. Mandi tried it on and it fit perfectly. Thelma was almost in tears. Thelma also gave Mandi pearl earrings and a necklace to not only wear for the occasion, but to keep with her always. They were one of the most expensive items Thelma ever owned, which she was now giving to Mandi. "You've earned it honey," Thelma told her.

Soon after, the wedding took place. This was a very memorable time for the entire Watkins family. On this day, they would all witness their daughter and sister finally become a wife, despite all the adversity she had been through. So this was very special for them.

Ronnie's siblings as well as his father, uncles and aunt were all in attendance. Though the entire event was somewhat bittersweet for him. All he could think about when his dad put on his suit jacket was his mother. How would she feel to witness her only boy finally getting married? *She would feel overjoyed*, he later answered to himself.

But after a moment, his father responded, saying, "She already is, son. She already is."

Afterwards, Ronnie hugged his father tight, patting him on the back, nearly dropping a tear. It was an emotional moment for both of them. Through the years, they had their ups and downs together as father and son, but at the end of the day, they both loved each other to death, and Willie sincerely believed that Mandi would make a good wife for his son.

"Well go get her son," Willie said to him. "You're already sure about this now, right? I mean… there's still time… "

Ronnie looked at his father for a moment, appearing a bit teary-eyed, shaking his head. "Naw," he answered. "I'll be fine. You always taught me to finish whatever I started… and I'm gonna do just that."

Willie couldn't have been more pleased. "My man. Then go get her," he said happily.

Mandi was also getting some last minute remarks alone with her father and mother. Afterwards, they hugged her as Thelma tapped Mandi on the back, encouraging her to be confident, telling her to take one day at a time and to trust that everything will be all right.

"I guess you won't be needin' these no mo'" Thelma joked while showing her daughter a sealed condom.

Mandi just laughed drying her eyes. "No mama. I'll be fine," she said.

"All right, now. That's my girl. Now go get me some grand-babies as fast as you can, ya hear? The soonuh, the bettuh. That's gone be yo' job fuh now… on top of yo' 'to do' list."

"I will mama. I will." she replied back, hugging her mother one final time.

About a half an hour later, the ceremony began. Mandi was beautiful. She wore the family wedding gown along with a relaxed hairstyle with a white headpiece attached to a veil covering her face.

Ronnie was equally as good looking. His hair sported waves, which were well defined when angled against the light. He had on a sharp tuxedo with a white flower in his left breast pocket along with shiny black shoes; the typical gentleman.

As he and Mandi stood side by side, they looked like a solid couple, with joy in their eyes and love in their hearts. Soon, the tradition came when the priest appeared before them, had each of them say their vows, exchange rings, and they were finally pronounced *Mr. and Mrs. Harris.*

Then, everyone clapped and later threw rice at the couple as they went outside to gather around to meet their families and take pictures, as the different family members went around to introduce themselves to each other.

A few hours later the reception was held at the church hall. It was a decent sized hall that accommodated everyone who came. The entrance had red carpet and midway to the end of the hall was a shiny wood floor, which also stood for the dance floor. On the carpeted area were a number of tables covered with white tablecloths and set with glasses and snacks. Mandi's parents had done an excellent job in arranging the event, and the couple was grateful.

As the reception commenced, there was music and entertainment and a host welcoming the couple as people began cheering with whistles and screams, bringing about that 'southern hospitality.' Even Ronnie was impressed. When it was finally time to dance, Ronnie brought his beautiful bride over as the two looked into each other's eyes, smiling. Music played throughout, filled with all kinds of memorable songs. Of all of them, their favorite was *The Closer I Get to You* by Roberta Flack and Donny Hathaway. It was as if that song was solely meant for them.

After the entire event ended, the newlyweds went down to Biloxi, Mississippi where they spent four nights together for their honeymoon. Mandi had never been to Biloxi before, but heard so many good things about it and begged Ronnie to go. At first, Ronnie objected to the idea, but later decided travelling there wasn't such a bad idea since it would give him further exposure to the South. Only twice had he traveled outside the state of Michigan. Therefore, going anywhere would give him a new perspective and broaden his horizons.

Plus, he was amazed by the attitude of people in Mississippi. To him, everyone was so down-to-earth and full of welcome compared to the people of the Midwest who appeared rather rude and indifferent at times.

When they got to Biloxi, they stayed in a hotel where they attended different restaurants and special events. There were casinos, fairs, circuses, and all kinds of fascinating places that instantly brought a smile to Ronnie's face. He was so happy he came. It was also then he became convinced that anywhere Mandi took him would end up becoming well worth his while.

During their four days there, they engaged in as much as they could absorb, as well as afford. Ronnie bought a Mississippi t-shirt for his dad and other local souvenirs, while Mandi, of course, shopped in the malls buying clothes, shoes and sunglasses. The couple also had their pictures taken there as a memory. It was the most exciting time of Ronnie's life. In his mind, Francine was right all along: Mandi was going to be a treasure in his life. And this was just the beginning. He never knew she could be so much fun to be around. It was a memorable honeymoon.

When they returned back to Detroit, Mandi moved all her things to Ronnie's new apartment that he had selected just weeks before the wedding. As usual, there was the rearranging of things to match their individual and collective tastes.

Soon after, Mandi began the process of pursuing a career in social work of some sort. She first chose to become a counselor in an inner city school so as to sense a feel of whether this was her calling. She applied at a number of schools throughout the city before finally being called for an interview.

She was later hired as a student counselor at a school called Wayne-McGregor Middle School. Initially, the job felt quite challenging due to her constant attention to numerous student issues and caseloads. But after the first quarter, things began becoming less overwhelming. Ronnie still had his freelance job as a home repairman, which brought in a stable income to where he was able to employ two workers.

After about four months into their marriage, Mandi found out she was pregnant. She was ecstatic. She was going to bring a new life into this world. Ronnie was happy too. When she told her parents about it, they instantly were elated, later commending Ronnie on a job well done. Francine, who was making a full recovery from her illness, was equally happy.

"Make sure you send me a picture once the baby's born," she would remind Mandi. Such a request was similar to when Mary Jo had asked the same of Francine.

By her eighth month at age 24, Mandi took a maternity leave from work. Though, neither she nor Ronnie wanted to know the baby's gender. They wanted it to be a surprise.

When it finally came time, Mandi was rushed to the hospital where she awaited labor. Her water broke suddenly, a couple days before expected. Ronnie, along with the nurses, were present during the process. After a strong battle, a baby began crying. It was a girl.

After the nurse cut the cord, she then placed the baby next to Mandi, who to her was the most precious thing she had ever seen. Mandi began crying. This was her baby. Ronnie, who was beside her, was very happy as well, staying in the room with Mandi until he was later assigned to leave the hospital for the evening. Before leaving however, he gave Mandi and the baby a sweet kiss, promising to return back the following day. Meanwhile, Mandi had to get plenty of rest.

When it was time to decide on a name, Mandi and Ronnie chose *Honey*. The name itself symbolized the 'sweet' joy the baby brought to both of them as well as a helpful reminder for them to always 'stick' together for the full development of the child. So *Honey* it was. A few days later, Mandi was discharged, carrying baby Honey in her arms while being wheeled off to Ronnie's car. Just like Thelma, Mandi was now a mother.

11

Pinky
Swear

MANDI EVENTUALLY SENT THE BABY PHOTOS TO HER
parents and Francine. They were all pleased with the
way Mandi's life had turned out. Francine was fully recovered
and beginning to move around on her own, which wasn't bad
for a woman of 70.

A month later, Mandi returned to school as a school
counselor. It was nice because the school year was only one
month from ending, which meant that soon she would be
able to get some more rest and spend her days with Honey.
She also decided to take the baby to visit her parents in Mississippi.

They ended up staying a week and a half there, because
Mandi's other siblings would later come to welcome the new-
est member of their family. She also informed Francine that
she was in town, and the two of them gathered with the baby
outside Francine's home. Then, after a few more days, Mandi

returned home to rejoin her husband, who had stayed behind to attend to his work.

A couple years would pass and Mandi became pregnant again, giving birth to another girl they named Daisy. By this time, Honey was almost 3. Ronnie hoped for a boy the next time around. He loved both his girls dearly, but having a boy would be marvelous, he thought.

In his mind, he couldn't wait one day to show his son his trade, along with telling him the steps of being a 'man.' He imagined having a son to wrestle with and play sports with, and all the other things his father did with him when he was a child. Mandi, who also wanted a son, made sure to write that goal in her dream book, envisioning a boy.

She became really hopeful but wanted to have a little rest before trying again. She had prayed about it and put in her goal book that she wanted only three children, so she believed for sure she would have a boy the next time. If it didn't happen, she wasn't going to worry, though. To her if it didn't happen the next time, the universe had its reasons, which would come out to her advantage, as she was taught by Francine.

So a couple years after Daisy was born, Mandi finally gave birth to a bouncing baby boy named Riley. Ronnie was so pleased, having kept his faith. As promised, Mandi was teaching Ronnie the power of the mind and how emotions constitute the process of attracting things into one's life. Ronnie was slowly coming to understand her lessons, but didn't partake in the reading of related books, complaining he was too busy. Though later he would end up joining Mandi in fully engaging in the material.

Yet for Mandi, her real interest was in impacting a stranger; someone who was totally unknown to her. To her, changing the life of someone she didn't know would be more powerful than helping someone she did know. From Francine's point of view, that brought more blessings and rewards than anything else. So she encouraged Mandi to do the best she could, stressing that soon the energy of the universe would show her a way.

By this time, Mandi had three children ages 6, 3 and 1. They had moved to a three-bedroom house that Ronnie and Mandi owned together in a quiet community. With it, came a two-car garage, a big front porch, an attic and a basement. To them, that felt good. Since it was financed, the couple had 20 years left to pay for it, which they weren't worried about.

The summer flew by, and soon it was already November. On one particular fall day, the weather was especially cold and icy. The wind was harsh and snow was falling randomly throughout the city of Detroit. The temperature was unusually cold for this time of year, hovering slightly below 10 degrees. Mandi appeared to be fighting with the wind, trying to get inside her house. She quickly got inside and shut the door behind her to shield herself from the cold air. The walkway was icy. She felt lucky she didn't fall. As much as she tried, adjusting to the cold Midwest weather was not easy for her. It was days like these when she missed the South.

As soon as she got in, she went upstairs to change into her warm sweater, sweat pants and long socks. She soon began making hot green tea. She had some time to stay home before picking Honey up from school, as a result of the sick day she used to get her car fixed. By the time she was settled, Mandi began sipping her tea, stirring it slowly before the phone rang.

She rushed over to pick it up. It was her father, Charlie. "Oh papa, how ya doin'? How's things down South?" she greeted.

"Not good. It's ya mama. She's sick."

"Wha... why what's wrong?"

"Doctuhs say she has colon cancuh and they want tuh do an operation on huh to have it removed."

Mandi was puzzled. "How... how soon?"

"Some time befo' the month is out. Yo' brothuhs and sistahs are all heah an' e'ryone out here is scared."

"Well how does mama feel?"

"She acts like she's okay but I can tell she's scared as all us."

"Do… do you want me to come home?"

"Could you? That would be appreciated dearly. She misses you. She really needs yo' help throughout all this. She always calls you her shining star—her angel."

"Well in a couple weeks is Thanksgiving. I can come then. Can ya'll still hol' on tuh then?"

"Of course we can, honey. In fact that's what we was hopin' on anyway. That would be the perfect time fo' the fam'ly. An' you can bring tha kids wit'ch ya too. You know we got plenty of room fo'em. So bring'em all. An' if ya could, bring Ronnie wit'ch ya too. Ya hear?"

"No problem papa. I'll make sure he comes along."

"Good. That's my girl. All right, you take ca'e now."

"All right papa. I will… and tell mama to hol' on naw and that I love huh. I'll be there soon."

"No problem, baby. I will."

"I love ya."

"Love ya too. See ya. Bye."

"Bye."

Mandi then hung up the phone. She suddenly was still, remaining silent on the couch until her tea got cold. But soon after, she caught herself, remembering to stay confident and joyous, believing that everything would turn out fine. She picked up Honey from school and the others from the daycare and hoped that Ronnie wouldn't object to the whole family going to Mississippi for Thanksgiving.

When she told him about her mother, Ronnie quickly agreed to go. He could see how important it was to his wife.

So on Wednesday before Thanksgiving, Mandi's family took off. As soon as they arrived, Charlie welcomed them at the airport and they returned to the home where Mandi spent her entire childhood. Thelma was resting in her bed, so everyone decided not to disturb her.

On the following day, all the family members came by and gathered around to have Thanksgiving dinner. It was an amazing time. There was of course the turkey with stuffing, sweet potato pie, plenty of roast beef, corn, rice, collard greens, potato salad, scrumptious blueberry pie and cheesecake, which only Thelma could make. It was her secret recipe that was revealed to Mandi when she was sick. Altogether, it was a delicious family meal that only the South could deliver. Even Ronnie enjoyed himself. Thelma, who was present with them, tried her best to savor the moment.

After dinner, just like with any other family feast, most of the members left, carrying with them their children and kissing Charlie and Thelma goodbye. When they left, the only people who were left were Mandi, her parents, Ronnie and their children. However, since everyone was exhausted, they chose not to discuss Thelma's condition until the following day. Mandi's family was going home Saturday. Therefore Friday was the only day they had left with ample time to talk.

When Friday came, Charlie decided it was best for Mandi and Ronnie to be alone with Thelma while he drove around town with the children. He figured that would relieve the conversation of distractions so that they could focus on what was serious. So that morning, Charlie took off with his grandchildren, leaving the three adults behind.

When he was gone, Mandi and Ronnie got dressed to talk with Thelma. Thelma, who was moaning periodically, lay flat on her bed. Beside her was a small end table that held a couple of medicine bottles and a glass of water. While in bed, she turned her head sideways and clenched her teeth as a result of the pain.

When Ronnie and Mandi came into her room, they could sense her agony and frustration.

"Mama, what's wrong?" Mandi cried.

"Oh... uh nothin', baby."

"What'ch ya mean nothing? You couldn't have dragged us all the way down here if nothing was wrong wit'ch ya. Mama, please... tell me."

Suddenly, Mandi acted like she was about to cry. Ronnie just stood still at the corner, silent. For a moment, this brought memories of his own mother, Dianne.

"Baby, please, sweetheart. Don't cry. Yo' mama's gonna be fine now, jus' fine. Ya hear?"

"But please tell me what's going on. I need to know. What's happening to your colon mama? I'm... *scared*."

Thelma paused for a minute. "Well alright. I'm not gone waste ya'll time any longuh. I might as well tell it tuh ya straight as it is. The truth is... I'm dyin'. The doctors say I got this colon cancuh and that they need to do an operation on me so I can have a shot at livin' longuh. They say though, that the operation is not guaranteed I'm gonna make it but it's better than any alternative I got so far. They say I have a 50/50 shot. That's how they put it."

"So what are these medications for?" Mandi asked.

"It's for controlling the problem... so that I don't feel the pain, I guess."

"You should know better not to take these. They're all toxins. They're part of the problem. They're not getting' you any better, ma. As your daughter, listen to me. Remember when I had cancer and Francine told me not to take any medication and just take raw fruits and vegetables. And look at me now. I am as healthy as can be."

"I know. I know. I guess I'm just so stubborn in my ways. That's all."

"Stop sayin' that. Do you want to live or not? Tell me, now. Do you want to leave me, papa, and everyone else here without ya? Huh, do ya?"

"No," she said flinching.

"Well listen to me. Please. I don't know what I'd do without you. Now, I was doin' a lil' research here, and I found the natural way to cure you of this disease is by you taking what is called a 'colon cleanse.' What it will do is help flush out any toxins in the colon that can bring you back to no'mal. Remembuh, that's what I did when I was sick. *Remembuh?*"

"I know sweety, but really… I… I jus' don't want to fight no mo', ya know?"

"So you wanna jus' *die* and leave us?"

"What I'm sayin' is that I just don't wanna fight no mo'. Whatevuh will be, will be. I… I'm jus' tiyad. Now I'm not sayin' I'm goin' to jus' stay here and die. I'm not sayin' that. I'm go'n do somethin' about it… and I decided… I decided that I'm gonna go on with the operation."

"No! Mama, please don't do it. Mama, please don't. Please mama! I know I've asked you for many things. But if there's one thing I'm beggin you, it's to not go on with this operation until at least you do this colon cleanse first and see how it turns out. If you do this one thing for me, I will never ever ask you to do another thing again. In fact, all the money I ever asked you in the past, I'll pay you back."

Thelma looked squarely at her daughter. "You foolish child, now you know you can nevuh repay yo' mama?"

"I know, mama."

Thelma got up to sit straight to talk with Mandi. Mandi then sat next to her mother on the bed and rested her head on Thelma's shoulder. "Listen child, I don't want you to cry. Look at me. C'mon look at me," Thelma commanded.

Mandi lifted her head and stared at her mother as she gently wiped her eyes.

"I want you to know that I am *so* proud of you. I really am. It had always been my dream to see you graduate, grow up, and have chil'ren. And thank God I got that chance. Me and yo' papa are so proud of you. I love you so much. But I don't want you to evuh feel bad. You still have a whole life ahead of you. I know I may not have been the best mama in the world, but Lord knows I tried raising ya'll as best I could. But you shouldn't cry. I'm very happy you're okay now and healthy. Okay?"

"But I don't want *you* to die mama."

Thelma smiled. "Baby, we all have our exits in life. So do you, ya know? It's part of life. I'm just glad I won't evuh have to bury you. That had always been my dream."

Though Mandi didn't want to hear that.

"Listen up. You'll always remember me, no matter where I go or what happens to me, right?"

Mandi nodded.

"Then I've never left. It's like Francine said: 'It's the thinking that makes it so.' Besides, there's nothin' wrong with death. All it is… is a transition. That's all. We're all eternal spirits, what I call 'a human experience.' I never went to school and know *that* at least."

"But it's still not the same mama. I wanna be able to feel you, to touch you, to hold you, to talk to you. I wanna hear you even when it doesn't make sense. At times, it may get on my nerves, but I don't mind hearing it again and again, jus' so I know you're still here wit' me. All of it would be music to my ears than to have you ever leave me."

Thelma gently rubbed Mandi's neck and ears. "I thank you for that baby… but I've lived a full life and have lived through so many things. I've been through the prohibition era, the world wars, the civil rights movement, leaders gettin' shot up and killed, on top of which I've experienced the greatest gift of all. I have had 11 children, seen 42 grandchil'ren, and 12 great-granchil'ren along with yo papa whom I've been married to fo' 45 years. And above all, I see you... in the flesh alive and well as can be. And, none of my chil'ren is in jail. Child, what mo' could I evuh ask fo'?"

"What about papa?"

Thelma thought for a moment, then laughed. "You know I'm go'n miss that man. I love him to death. I really do. We had some great times together... even before you was born."

Mandi then cracked a smile. Soon, Thelma remembered what she had wanted to tell Mandi that was so important. "Now listen Mandi, if you want to make yo' mama really proud, you wanna know what you can do fo' me?"

Mandi nodded. "Yes, anything mama. What is it?"

"Now get out yo' right hand with yo' pinky stickin' out."

Mandi did and suddenly Thelma brought her right pinky finger out and used it to hook Mandi's pinky finger grabbing it close to her, looking in Mandi's eyes.

"Now you know what Francine gave you was a gift. It's called a second chance on life."

Mandi nodded.

"Okay, well I want you to promise me that you're gonna do exactly what Francine told you. You're gonna share with someone or some people the secret about the law 'a attraction and how to apply it. I don't mean yo' husband Ronnie or yo' chil'ren. Tuh me, those're all selfish reasons. But I want it to be for some stranger or person you've nevuh seen befo' willin' to learn. The favor was carried on to Francine, which is now carried on to you. Now you have to carry it on to someone else, and in time, they will pass it on to someone else. That's the only favuh I will ever ask of you to do fo' me, 'cause I already know you'll do everything else. But if there's one favor I will ever ask of you, it's this one. You never know whose life you'll change. Now promise me you'll do it."

Mandi's eyes watered as she stared close to her mother. "I promise mama."

"Pinky promise?"

"I pinky *swear*, mama. I swear I must... and I *will*. A promise is a promise, and I'll never break that... *ever.*"

"No matter how long it takes?"

"No matter how long it takes. I will. You never quit on me. So I *won't* quit on you."

Thelma looked at her daughter closely. "I trust you child. I know you'll do it. Now give yo' mama a hug."

They then hugged real tight which had Ronnie feeling very emotional.

Thelma then added, "Baby I want you to know somethin'. I believe you have the gift of a great teacher. I can see it in ya. You have that talent to grab people's attention and really teach. I know I've never told you that befo', but... you do. And I want you to use that when teaching this secret, ya hear?"

"Yes ma'am."

"I thank ya child. I thank ya."

Suddenly, Thelma turned to Ronnie. "Child c'mere. Come to yo' *othuh* mama. Come sit right next to me," she told him.

Ronnie went over and sat beside her.

"How ya doin'?" she smiled at him.

"Good... *mama.*"

Both Thelma and Mandi laughed. "Au, that's good, son. Now listen, I have some instructions I want tuh give you fo' me. So make sho' you never forget them, ya hear? 'Cause it's important. I mean serious business."

"Yes ma'am."

"Good."

Thelma looked Ronnie squarely in the face. "Now I know I may talk a lil' crazy sometimes, but forgive me. It's nothin' personal. It's jus' the way I am sometimes. Okay?"

"Okay."

"Now what I need fo' you to do is this... take good care of my daughter. I love her so much. She's my shining star, my sunshine, my angel. She's the reason I always wake up every mo'nin', saying: '*Thank you Jesus.*' So take care of her. I already know you'll take care of the chil'ren, yo' business, and e'rything else, but *please*... take care of her. I know you all may get into the arguin' and fussin' and fightin' and all that, but make sho' you work it out. Sometimes, it may take a lil' time but one thing I know fo' sho', is that talkin' it over all the time is what will keep ya'll afloat. From my experience, God and communication is very important, ya hear? It's key."

Ronnie nodded

"Because I'm a tell you somethin'," Thelma continued. "There's been times me and Charlie would get on each other's nerves. Mandi'll tell you. There's been times I would get so heated that I would just wanna ring his neck. But in the end... I love that man tuh death and wouldn't want to trade him for anyone or anything else in the world, 'cause I love him that much. And I mean that. Only death could keep me from that man, let me tell ya. And that's what's kept us together for so long. Love. You can see, we don't have a great big fancy house, but we do have each other... and that's okay with me. Lord knows me and him done messed up e'rything there is in the book. I mean we even misspelled Mandi's name for Christ's sake. But through thick and thin, good times and bad, we still stuck together... kind a like the Kennedys, John and Bobby. So I'm tellin' ya'll to hold on tight. She needs you. And you need her... *I hope.* So don't ever *ever* break that vow. Okay?"

"Okay."

"Promise me."

"I promise."

Thelma then pulled out her right pinky finger. "Pinky promise?"

"I pinky swear," Ronnie answered pulling out his right pinky finger, hooking it up to hers.

"My son," she smiled.

They then hugged and soon both Mandi and Ronnie expressed to Thelma utmost gratitude for her unconditional love. "I want you to know something too mama… I love you." Ronnie said. "You remind me so much of my mama."

"I love you too, baby," she replied back. "Just be good to my daughter, now. You do that fo' me, and we'll be *all* right."

Later, Mandi and Ronnie waited outside for Charlie's return. As they were waiting, Mandi leaned against Ronnie's shoulder as he wrapped his arms around caressing her forehead. Ronnie turned to her. "Baby," he said, looking at her.

"Yes," she answered.

"Thank you for this trip. I needed it."

"You're welcome, baby," she smiled. "Thank you for coming."

"You're welcome."

By the following day, the family had arrived back to Detroit. For the next couple months, everything went smoothly. Then in late February, Mandi got that dreadful phone call from her dad. Thelma had died.

According to Charlie, she didn't survive the operation, claiming that the cancer had grown too far past her colon and into other organs. Plus, since she was 65, the entire procedure was risky to begin with. However it was what Thelma wanted.

Mandi fell to the floor after hearing the news, sobbing, unable to even hold the phone. Ronnie, who was in the basement doing some laundry, heard her and went over to console her.

Eventually after the ordeal, it was agreed that Mandi would go alone to her mother's funeral. Francine, who also heard the news, was going to be there as well. With it being so sudden, it seemed short notice for the entire family to suddenly follow her to pay their last respects. Plus, the finances to send the whole family to and fro were not there. However, Ronnie would have liked to have gone.

When Mandi arrived, she hugged her siblings, as they all were in tears. She and Francine also shared a tight hug.

"I wouldn't have missed this for the world. She was so very dear to me," Francine said.

"I know," replied Mandi.

During the funeral, Mandi took the podium to make some comments about Thelma. She spoke with a passion like no one else. Everyone in her family was impressed. They never knew she could deliver such a powerful statement about her mother like that.

After the funeral was over, Darin, her brother, pulled her to the side. "You know that thing you said about mama was really good. Who taught you how to speak like that?"

"I don't know. It just flowed naturally, I guess. Must've been probably from the books I've read through the years."

"Well… mama definitely knew what she was talkin' 'bout. She always said you had the gift for public speaking. She said that you had that magnetic ability to attract a crowd. So keep it up. That was good."

"Thanks brother," she said. "You're a blessing too, you know that?"

"Thanks sis, you are too. You are too."

"By the way," Mandi remarked. "I finally did catch a butterfly… back when I was 13."

Darin smiled. "I know," he said.

Mandi was a little surprised to hear that. Normally, she would expect Darin to challenge her by proving it, like their childhood days.

"Wait… how?"

"Who else? Mama of course. She told me all about it when you two were at Francine's home. At first I didn't believe her, but if God was able to save you from cancer, what other miracles couldn't He do?"

Afterwards, the two siblings hugged each other tight.

"I'll always love you," she told him.

"I've never stopped," he said.

Afterwards, Darin looked at his sister one more time, winked at her, then turned around to mingle with the crowd. From hearing what he said about her ability to speak, Mandi suddenly remembered again the promise she had made to her mother.

When she returned back to Detroit, she decided to fully pursue mentoring someone interested in success principles through the law of attraction. That now became her mission, her goal, her obsession—which of course she wrote in her dream book and beside it, she wrote in parentheses: (*For Mama*).

12

⧼⧽

Something Priceless

THE FOLLOWING YEAR, MANDI CHOSE TO ESTABLISH relationships with the students who came to her with their personal problems. She tried her best to listen attentively to what they had to say. If there were conditions back home or in their personal lives they wanted addressed, she listened. However, a good number of the students who she listened to often wailed about their problems as if they were in therapy.

Having ten siblings, Mandi was careful not to get too emotionally attached to the students for the possibility that they may be wasting her energy and time. The students at Wayne-McGregor Middle School were mostly between 11 and 14 years old, so to her, they were the perfect age to be introduced to the law of attraction. If coached correctly, they could be empowered to look at life a lot more clearly and to go far with their ambitions rather than be held captive mentally.

In the corner of Mandi's office was a small stack of different books on growth development that Francine had recommended for her to read, and which she read periodically over and over again. By this time, Ronnie began to read them too and started telling Mandi how it changed his whole outlook on life. Yet, he encouraged Mandi to be careful exposing them to certain people and to be cautious of the bureaucracy that existed in the public school system. He was well aware that more school problems were caused by administrators who were more focused on getting 'funding' and less on the low test scores and illiteracy levels, especially in urban schools. Those problems often enabled more funding, so the kids may have plenty of new books to read, but the school's literacy levels were still low. He warned Mandi that if she encouraged or brought about too much success with her teachings, the school could lose funding, and she could possible lose her job.

It was because of this that Ronnie quit school. Early on, he felt that the school he was in just didn't provide the means he needed to 'succeed.' To him, all the school did was fill his time with useless information he would never use or need in life, such as dissecting a frog or understanding the FOIL method in mathematics. They were pure boredom to him. School just never excited him enough or motivated him enough to want to continue.

Mandi listened very attentively to Ronnie, but still believed in the powers of the universe and felt that it would eventually bring someone to her who was willing to accept her as their mentor. And it was also what she indicated in her dream book.

As months passed, Mandi, who was now 33, began lending books to certain students whom she felt were sincere in wanting to read them. And as a result, she got back a few mixed reviews. Some of the students never returned to her office while others kept postponing reading the books. When she asked for them back, some would not return them or they would keep making excuses, nearly shunning her away, making fun of the process. Yet she did get the books back from some of the students who read them.

For those who did read them, many commented that they were the best books they had ever read and thanked her immensely for sharing them. This was exactly what they needed. Hearing such news was music to her soul. Many would eventually go on to get their own personal copies.

Though, other results became more damaging. Some ignorant parents of those same students would storm into her office, interrogating her as to why she was lending out such material and what business it was of hers to do so. The school principal was immediately notified of this, and deemed the entire process unreasonable and inappropriate. The explanation was that since such materials were not part of the school curriculum, they were not necessary for students. But when Mandi questioned what the students were actually learning (since over 60 percent of them still read at a third grade level), the principal would not respond, since she didn't know the answer.

It was apparent that the only thing that the school was interested in, like most urban schools, was funding rather than fixing the problems and addressing the real issues. This was why some well-meaning teachers either switched careers or ended up doing the minimal effort to earn a salary, since they were hardly rewarded for putting in their 'all.' This was especially the case when Mandi considered that most teachers' pay was only 35 percent above minimum wage. With a salary like that and having to invest hours outside the school to make ends meet, how could any teacher be motivated to serve anyone or do anything properly?

People generally react to incentives, and the schools were not rewarding their teachers to devote more effort and time into the students, which in turn ensures a failed system. Teaching involves sacrifice, away from family and sleep sometimes, and all most teachers want is to be appreciated more, which is through better pay and not having to personally invest their own money in school supplies and classroom equipment. When those things are lacking, it is so easy for frustration and tension to build within the staff, if they don't quit first.

It then became apparent to Mandi how and why the average individual never learned about the law of attraction, much less knew what it was. Even Francine's mentor told Francine the same thing. All of a sudden, Mandi began to make sense of the system. It was all a game. It had very little if anything at all to do with the welfare of the students. It was all about the money. Simply put, the more problems the school could invent, the more money they'd receive from the state and local government as a means of 'fixing' the problem, which of course would never get done. The whole emphasis was on managing the problem, not getting rid of it.

The principal, Mrs. Saunders, along with a couple state officials and school board members eventually set up a meeting with Mandi in a private office to discuss her practices before briefing her again on her actual duties and job responsibilities as a school counselor—in case she didn't quite understand.

According to them, as a counselor she was to schedule classes for the students while seeing them periodically concerning their grades, if they needed attention. Anything beyond that was not required. She was not a doctor or therapist, and if she were, according to them, she was to prescribe medications for students as needed, which she needed a degree for anyway. To Mandi this was all completely absurd and ludicrous.

Judging from experience, Mandi determined that a troubled student should first be examined to discover what's causing the trouble, which could be for many reasons. For instance, his parents might be going through a divorce, or his mother might be sick, or there's verbal abuse in the home, or the father just lost his job, or his family is losing their home, or he's being bullied at school, etc... The possibilities are endless. Once the root cause is found, there are therapies that can be put into place to correct that problem. But to simply say it's a deficit of a specific medication that is causing the behavior as a need to reverse the situation, is a sick concept that makes absolutely no sense, she thought, since the *real* cause still exists.

After hearing them go on for about two hours, Mandi agreed she would cease from distributing any books or success materials. If she chose to continue, she would be suspended, and eventually fired. Without the staff saying a word, Mandi already knew that they would send out students as 'spies' to report back whether or not she continued such practices. But what upset Mandi the most was when one of the members of the board asked why she would even concern herself that much with the students. The message was, that she had her own family of her own to take care of and should concentrate on just doing her job and going home.

Before the meeting was over, Mandi had already made up her mind to look for another job by the end of the school year. How could she fulfill her promise to her mother by living under such constraints? To her, that wasn't living. That was surviving. And she didn't want to just survive. She wanted to *live*.

For the sake of a salary, many other teachers before Mandi, decided to change their work ethic and dance to the school music. But Mandi refused to participate. Of course, there was the mortgage and other family expenses that had to be paid, but with the right mindset, Mandi believed that a way would be made for her to freely teach the law of attraction. She just had to trust it and believe in it, and the universe would deliver.

During May of that school year, Mandi called Francine, asking if she could spend a day with her during the summer to explain her ordeal. Francine welcomed the idea. A big break from Michigan was exactly what Mandi needed anyway. She was delighted.

When she went to tell Ronnie her plans, Ronnie didn't mind. However, he was concerned about who would take care of the kids since he was constantly working. Mandi in return agreed to take them with her to Mississippi to spend time with her father, which was a great idea since he was all by himself now. Company with the children would definitely cheer him up, she thought.

The maximum time that Mandi wanted to stay there was a month. That way, it would give her a lot of room to relax, reevaluate things and gain a fresh start on her career through wisdom from Francine. She promised Ronnie she would call everyday to see how he was doing.

Ronnie agreed and within a week after school was over, Mandi went down South with the children once again to revisit her roots. Charlie was so delighted to see them. By this time however, he had gotten a little heavier and drank a little more as a means of 'coping' with Thelma's absence. He missed her. Yet, he was still full of life and energy and still knew how to make everyone smile.

During the first week, Mandi spent a considerable amount of time with her father, talking about life, among other things. It was the first time Mandi spent a lot of time with him since Thelma died, which brought tears to his eyes. His other children, most of whom lived within 20 miles from him, rarely found time to visit, which caused him to feel lonely and depressed at times. The only time he was ever remembered it seemed was when his children needed him to watch their kids.

The only one who still dropped by regularly was Carla, who was now the sole owner of *Thelma's Secret*. By now, the bakery had become a thriving business with a very reputable name throughout Skeegee County, serving many families and individuals who always came for more pastries and delicious cakes. It appeared that what Thelma started was blessed from the beginning. One didn't need much education to pursue a dream, since the dreams themselves were the most powerful.

Yet, when Charlie was with Mandi, he finally saw a reason for living again. It made him feel that he was still important. And spending time with her father gave Mandi the ability to learn about another side to him as he learned about her. Therefore, it was a precious time neither of them would forget. They shared plenty of laughs and tears, which made Mandi almost not want to return to Detroit. There were just some things about family life and her hometown that brought her such calmness and peace of mind.

Yet, she wasn't going to focus on her return. She wanted to soak in every minute she had with her father, enjoying in the moment. Since he was getting old, Mandi didn't know when she would have this much time to spend with him again. So she wanted to make this visit count and make the best of it. She understood that the best time to spend with anyone was when they were living, not when they were dead.

Midway through her vacation, Mandi decided that it was time to call on Francine. By this time now, Francine was 79. Therefore there was no telling how many more times Mandi would see her again. Yet, from what she heard, Francine was still energetic, living life in a perfect stride.

When she got there, the maid opened the door for her, bringing her to the guest house where Francine awaited her as servants brought special food, placing it on a glass table as Mandi anticipated. She had skipped breakfast at her father's house before coming to see Francine, because she knew how hospitable Francine was. Francine welcomed Mandi with open arms. And knowing that Mandi was coming, Francine had prepared some priceless items for Mandi to take with her.

"You know Mandi, you are by far one of the best students I have ever had and I want you to know how much I appreciate your energy and undying spirit, despite all that you've been through."

"Thank you, but I have *you* to thank. I never would have been here without you."

"Yes of course, but always remember, it was you who *chose* to go this route, which is something no one can do by force."

"That *is* true."

"So again, I salute you. Now, I want to discuss the issues that I need to discuss first. You know as well as I do that despite everything, I *am* getting older. It's a fact I've got to face. I don't know how much longer I will remain in this body before seeing my dear John again. In fact, no one knows. However, I wouldn't want to depart from this world without seeing you again before collecting some gifts I have for you. They're priceless items, worth more than all the gold, diamonds, rubies and platinum of this world put together."

Mandi, a bit anxious, began to ask what she was speaking of.

But without answering, Francine ordered one of the maids to bring about a small black suitcase that was tucked beneath her bed. Minutes later, the maid returned with a bag.

"Thank you, Catherine," Francine said.

Francine then gave the bag to Mandi. "Go 'head open it up," Francine told her.

Mandi did. What she saw was a series of books bound together with rope. Excitedly she untied the rope.

"Aw... 'Think and Grow Rich' by Napoleon Hill!" she shouted, pulling it out. "And you have, 'The Magic of Thinking Big' by David Schwartz. Plus you have, 'The Magic of Believing' and 'The Power of Positive Thinking'... "

"That's right, that's right," Francine stated. "I packaged all those books for you. Those are all the books I've read and re-read to enrich my soul, which I now pass onto you. They're yours now. These books are powerful, Mandi. They will enrich your life and are the techniques needed for you to persevere in every endeavor and path you so wish. Once read and applied, they will create magic in your life and produce abundance."

"Aw Francine, thank you. I do appreciate it. Trust me, I do. These types of books are what will keep me focused in the direction I want to go which will help with my vibration."

"That's exactly right. Always read them and take at least one with you everywhere. May they help you become a better person and use them to share with others around you. Now there are a few extras which you may not have heard of that I included there, which are just as good if not better."

Mandi went over to hug her. "Francine, I just don't know what to say."

"Just say that you'll expose what you've been taught to others, enriching their lives as well. It can't be just your family, but anyone who's coachable and willing to learn. Just like you've been a great follower, I know you'll make a great leader."

"Thank you. And I promise to be just that."

"Good girl. You know Mandi, I trust you. Really I do. It's amazing how much you've grown to become the wonderful woman you are now. You have always been one of my best students. You never objected or challenged me even once. You always listened and accepted with trust, then applied the principles... *kinda like how I did with my mentor, but...* what I also discovered was that since you first visited me, you never once asked me for money or hinted that you were in need of anything tangible, which I admire. That shows you're truly a woman of character, and I'm very proud of that."

"Thank you."

"No problem, but it's the truth though, and I want you to know that. You are a rare breed, indeed. Virtually anyone else who ever came through this house, always came for some financial support. Whether it was a 50/50 partnership deal, investments, or for me just to always loan them money, it didn't matter. It was just always about business. That's where it started and that's where it ended. Other than that, my existence to them meant nothing. If plagued with a situation, they weren't there."

Francine suddenly went over to a nearby end table that had a drawer. She pulled out the door and inside, grabbed an envelope before placing it on the glass table.

"You have no idea how much it meant to me when you came down to see me when I had leukemia. That meant a whole lot, which is why I am honored to call you my dear friend, and why I'm giving you *this*. Go ahead, open it," she commanded.

Mandi went and opened the envelope. "A check for fifty thousand dollars!" she yelled.

"That's right. You earned it. I... "

Mandi then went over and squeezed Francine so tight. She just couldn't contain herself. The emotion was just more than she could bear that she nearly broke down crying. This was exactly the break she needed.

"Thank you!" she said again.

"You're welcome, but as I was saying, I've realized that my time here on earth is getting shorter and shorter now and I've been working on how to dispose of all my assets, like Andrew Carnegie did. He once said that a man who dies rich, dies disgraced. So, some of my money I've sent to different foundations and charities. Even schools have received part of my money as well as agencies that offer scholarships. My mission is to help as many people and groups as I can that deserve it because if there's one thing for sure that I know of, it's this: You can't take any of this with you, no matter how hard you try. So it's best that I use what I have and help mankind because my life has been an exciting adventure and I've learned so much and have figured that if I was able to impact one life as I was impacted, then my trip here on earth was well worth it. And I know deep down that if Mary Jo were still here, she would feel mighty proud that I kept my word."

"She *is* here," replied Mandi. "And you can feel rest assured knowing that I will carry on her dream in sharing this with someone else too."

Francine couldn't have been more pleased. That was probably the sweetest sentence she had ever heard Mandi say.

"I know you will. But try and impact at least one life, okay? That's all I ask. And with that money, I want you to use part of that possibly as capital for your husband's business, you can use it to support your dad while the rest, you use to pay for any expenses with your family until you finally find an environment you can work in and operate more freely in getting the message across."

Mandi was shocked. "So you remembered what I said to you on the phone about quitting my job in search of a better opportunity?"

"Sweetheart, I may be old but I listen to everything. I understand your struggle. And it's not easy, I know. The system is rigged in ensuring that no one is free. My mentor, Mary Jo, use to tell me about the same problem she had. But remember never to give up on finding someone. You never know who you'll impact, which can add huge dividends to your life. The right student will come along at the right place and right time, never to abandon you and he or she will always cherish and love you forever. It'll be like magic. You'll see. What you put forth, you get back. It's the law of nature."

Mandi went over to hug her once more. Soon after, Francine began talking small talk again until it was finally time for Mandi to go.

"Take care my child. I bid you good luck in your life and use that money wisely."

"I will. I will."

However, just before Francine could shut the door, Mandi remembered something important... Actually, it was an offer.

"Oh... please before I go, I just remembered something. It's something that I need so that I remember you existed in my life."

Francine looked puzzled. "What is it?" she asked.

"Can we *please* take a picture together, just you and me? After all this time we've been together, we've never ever done that. And it would mean so much to me if we did, just once," she said.

Francine thought for a moment. "Oh you know what, you're right. I don't know why I never thought of that. Must be ol' age, I guess. Anyway stay right here."

"Catherine! Catherine!" Francine yelled.

Within minutes, Catherine appeared. "Yes?" she asked.

"Go get me my camera. I want you to take a few pictures of me and Mandi together."

"Yes ma'am."

Mandi smiled.

Soon after, Catherine came with the camera and Francine and Mandi went outside to take pictures. Catherine was actually a real professional at snapping photos and willfully chose certain spots around the villa to capture the two of them. It made for a very interesting scene. Before long, she got out of control and began snapping as many as 32 shots in all different settings.

"Okay, that's enough Catherine," Francine said finally. "Thank you so much. You are a great photographer."

Catherine then smiled, giving the camera back to Francine and left.

Francine shook her head. "I don't know what got into her."

"Me neither," Mandi smiled.

"Anyway, I'm gonna have these developed and send them off to you in Detroit."

"If it's not a problem, could you send a few also to my papa here? I'm sure it would mean so much to him too."

Francine smiled. "Sure thing. Will do."

Afterwards, the two of them hugged one more time remaining in deep emotion together. Catherine, who could see them through the window of the house, also felt emotional. She didn't know what it was, but in her heart, knew that whatever bond Francine and Mandi shared had to be so precious; it was above all the money in the whole wide world.

13

Francine

MANDI WAS SO ECSTATIC ABOUT THE GIFT FRANCINE gave her that she couldn't contain herself. When she arrived back to see her father, she rushed over to hug him tight. Charlie was a bit surprised.

"I love you papa," she told him.

"I love you too baby, but... but what's the special occasion? I haven't seen you this happy since you found out you was gettin' married. It seems like every time you come back from Francine's house, magic just happens outta nowhere."

Mandi stood still and glanced at him. At that moment, Honey, who was now 9, grabbed her mother's left arm. "Yeah mom, why're you so happy all of a sudden?" she wondered.

"Kids," she said with joy. "Your daddy's gonna finally have that business he always wanted to get off the ground."

"Really, how?" Honey asked.

"I just got a check of $50,000 from Francine!"

Everyone roared with excitement. Even Charlie began to dance some moves like he did in the old days.

"Papa, I want you from this point on not to sit here feeling sorry fo' yo'self. I want you to travel. Go to places like Biloxi or the Grand Canyon. Visit the Niagara Falls. You've been here far too long. It's now time for you to finally explore. Live your life! You know mama would want that."

Charlie smiled. "My baby," he said, giving her a hug and kiss. "I'll do that, ya hear? Deep down, I always wanted to do that."

"Well now's yo' chance. Go out and enjoy life."

"Just make sho' that check clears when you get home. Okay? Don't lose it."

"With the quickness, papa," Mandi replied. "With the quickness."

Charlie then pulled her off to the side, alerting the grandchildren to step back. "So, how much am I gettin'?" he whispered.

"Uh…I was thinkin' 17. $17,000."

Just then Charlie went and hugged Mandi so much and kissed her, shaking her hand.

"That'll do!" he shouted. "That'll *do.*"

He then paused and added another point. "Ya know quiet as kept, yo' mama always wanted me to tell you this… and I agree too with her. But if you tell anyone, I'll deny it, ya hear?"

Mandi nodded. "I undastand. What is it?" she asked.

"Well… out of all our chil'ren, you were always her favorite. Mine too. You always had so much promise and hope in you than all the others. I love ya. I jus' wanted you to know that, but don't go off tellin' yo' brothers and sisters now, ya hear? This is our little secret… jus' between you and me."

Mandi looked at him in shock. "That's it?" she wondered. "In truth, papa, I already *knew* that."

"Really? How so?"

"Out of all the girls that got married, mama never gave her precious pearl earrings and necklace fo' any of 'em to keep… except me."

Charlie smiled. "My baby," he said. "By the way also, I already made out a will for you to have this property once I'm gone."

"But papa, what will the others get?"

"Don'tch you worry about that. I already thought of somethin'. It might not be as much as you got but they'll get somethin'… if they still remembuh me."

"Aw papa, don't worry. They will. Anyway, let's not focus on that right now. Let's take the kids off and celebrate."

"You know… you're right. You're right about that. C'mon, let's go."

Suddenly Charlie turned around, seeing his glass of beer spilt from the table onto the porch.

"Grandpa, it wasn't my fault," Honey said. "I told Daisy not to touch it and she wouldn't listen and tipped it over."

Charlie looked at the entire incident and laughed. "You know don't even worry about it dear, because from now on, yo' *grandpa* here, don't drink *no* mo'. I'm goin' on vacation tuh see the world!"

The children all cheered while Mandi smiled.

When Mandi and the children returned back home, Ronnie greeted them at the airport, wearing his usual Michigan Wolverines baseball cap. Still consumed by emotion, Mandi just grabbed him, giving him a big hug and kiss, which had the children saying, *"Eeeew! Gross!"*

Mandi went on to explain about the money Francine gave her as well as the books and other things. Ronnie was so excited because that money was actually the extra capital he needed to start his construction company. However Mandi made it clear that he was only going to get $17,000. The other

$17,000 would go to her father while the remaining $16,000 would cover the expenses of the household until she was able to find a job where she could carry out her mission.

In the meantime, she was going to devote her energy toward reading all the books Francine gave her. Mandi felt that an idea would come to her to help her figure out how to carry out her mission.

Within the coming months, Mandi gave her father the money she promised him, which he used for travelling. His first trip was to the Grand Canyon, and from there, who knows what was next. But as Mandi once told him, "Go as far as you can see, and when you there, you'll see more."

Charlie took that principle to light and decided to enjoy his life and let life show him whatever it was going to. He suddenly was into adventure and for once, wanted to now live life on his own terms, so long that he was healthy and safe. So throughout his journey, he traveled in his car with his sunshades on while a picture of Thelma hung on his rear view mirror.

As time went on, Ronnie's business, *Ron's Home Repair,* was starting to pick up. He employed five people, had a big truck, and started to get bigger contracts with different companies to work for. Therefore more and more income kept coming into the home, which was always a good feeling.

Throughout this time, Mandi was a stay at home mom and continued reading continued reading the books Francine gave her. She highlighted many topics and diligently wrote down some of the major points in a separate notebook in order to instantly refer to them when needed. There was so much 'meat' in all of the books that there was no way one could remember and apply all of the elements after reading them just one time. The concepts that were covered required a reader to refer back time and time again.

Mandi understood one principle. If she was going to be a leader, she had to be a reader. The most influential and powerful people throughout history were all readers. A man who will not read is no better off than a man who cannot read. Napoleon Bonaparte, who was regarded by many as one of the greatest generals and commanders of all time, made a powerful statement, which was this:

"The only right way of learning the science of war, is to read and reread the campaigns of the great captains."

Napoleon became one of the greatest military captains in history. This statement would later be quoted by World War II General and Naval Officer, George Smith Patton Jr., who later became a great commander in his own right as a result of his great leadership skills and outspokenness.

Simply put, leaders read!

This in turn, would explain to Mandi why the school system was comfortable with not properly educating its students. There's power in reading and if the students all knew how to read, then many problems would cease from the school, and it would lose the major funding it needed *for* these 'problems.' This would also explain as to why a lot of affluent families who know the score, home school their children. They understand already that the present school system is broken.

How interesting the country would be if there was a law passed that commanded all students to just read *Think and Grow Rich* before they could enter the fifth grade, thought Mandi. But the problem is that it would create thinkers, and thinkers can be threatening to any establishment whose sole desire is to control them.

Is it any wonder why students in the United States are (in most cases) dead last in passing vital subjects that students in Third World countries excel in? As a result, these same foreigners later become high achievers in their own field, owning businesses and commanding authority while in the United States.

Francine gave Mandi 15 books. They were:

Title	Author
The Magic of Thinking Big	*David J. Schwartz*
How to Win Friends and Influence People	*Dale Carnegie*
The Power of Positive Thinking	*Norman Vincent Peale*
The Greatest Salesman in the World	*Og Mandino*
See You at the Top!	*Zig Ziglar*
Hung by the Tongue	*Francis P. Martin*
As a Man Thinketh	*James Allen*
The Magic of Believing	*Claude M. Bristol*
The Science of Getting Rich	*Wallace Wattles*
The Science of Being Great	*Wallace Wattles*
Think and Grow Rich	*Napoleon Hill*
The Law of Success in 16 Lessons	*Napoleon Hill*
How to Have Power and Confidence in Dealing with People	*Les Giblin*
Psycho-cybernetics	*Maxwell Maltz*
Success Through a Positive Mental Attitude	*W. Clement Stone, Napoleon Hill*

Almost six months after returning from Mississippi, Mandi had completed 10 books. She was halfway through reading *Success Through a Positive Mental Attitude* by Napoleon Hill and W. Clement Stone, when the phone rang.

Mandi put the book upside down and rushed over to see who it was. It was her sister, Carla. "Hey sis, what's shakin' down South? How's business?" asked Mandi.

"Aw business is good," she said. "Actually, it's nevuh been better. In fact, I'm in the works of finding another building to expand and need more staff. So thanks for askin'. But the reason I called was to give you some news… an update, rather."

"Is it papa?" she wondered.

"Naw. Actually papa's fine. He's enjoyin' life, I guess. Livin' it up. He even lost a bit a weight last time I saw him. He's so happy now."

Mandi was relieved.

"I just wanted to tell you that… Francine passed."

Mandi closed her eyes. For a moment, there was silence.

"Hello, are you still there?" asked Carla.

Mandi cleared her throat. "Yes, I'm here. Did they say what happened?"

"Not really. All they could say was that she died in her sleep. Therefore they ruled it as natural cause. She was 80, which ain't bad at all. It was strange though, because according to the people, they found her with a smirk on her face... while holdin' a frame of her husband, John, in her arms. From what I heard, she missed him a lot."

"She died peacefully, then. She's now home. When is the wake?"

"This Friday at Wilson's Funeral Home, at 9 in the mo'nin'. Why, you comin'?"

"Hell yeah I'm comin'! The reason we're even on this phone is because of her."

"Yeah I know."

Carla then remembered something else. "Oh and one more thing," she said.

"What is it?"

"I've got the latest news on a very special person; a person you might like to know about."

"Who?"

"Well I'll give you a hint. He was a high school crush."

Mandi didn't have to think twice. "Fletcher," she replied.

"Yup, you guessed it."

"Damn it Carla... what'ch you do that fo'? You *know* I've moved on. I could care less now."

There was a moment of silence again.

"So what happened?" asked Mandi.

"Well... apparently, he's been in trouble with the law several times. He has five felonies and right now's in jail for assault and attempted murder on his girlfriend. At least that's what everyone else is saying. But since this isn't his first case, he may be going to jail for a good while... like at least 10 years or so."

"Where's he now?"

"Skeegee County Jail."

"For how long?"

"About two months now. He's still awaiting his fate. His bond is set at $150,000."

Mandi tried to think for a moment. "Well why didn't you bother to tell me this before?"

"*Beeecause* first off, you're married. That's number one. Number two, you have a family. And thirdly, even if I did, I know you wouldn't come all the way down here just to come see him for just 30 minutes or so. But I guess since Francine's passed, you may have a reason to finally stop by after all... since... you're coming here, right?"

As much as this was a sad moment, inside, Mandi felt excited, as if the universe was giving her an opportunity of some sort. Though, she wasn't sure yet what it was. She just could feel it. "I will... but Carla you got to promise me something."

"Sure. What is it?"

"You know I have never begged you for anything that wasn't important."

"I know. So what's up?"

"Please tell no one of this, please. Not your husband, no one. Not even papa or anyone else in our family."

"I promise, I won't."

"You swear?"

"I pinky swear."

"Good. Now, is it possible you can go over the county jail and reserve my name for Friday somewhere between the hours of 12 and 2 p.m. so I can visit him? Please."

"Why?'

"It's just important. I can feel it."

"Girl, you gotta do better than that. How come?"

Mandi was a bit agitated with the question.

"Just think of it as… female intuition. Okay? You wouldn't be tellin' me this if it wasn't fo' a reason, and I have to find out what that reason is. So I'm beggin' you, can you please do that fo' me?"

There was no answer.

"Okay, I promise to give you mama's blueberry cake recipe for the bakery."

"Now you're talkin'. See, that's all you had to say. Not a problem."

"Thanks. You're a sweetheart. I'll fly over there and be there by Wednesday, okay?'

"Okay."

"Oh and uh Carla darlin'?"

"Yes?"

"Thank you so much. You have no idea how the magic of this moment is going to bring marvelous results for me. I can feel it."

"Uh… okay," she said, appearing confused. "Don't worry 'bout it. Besides, we're family, remember? That's just what we do here."

Mandi smiled. "Thanks sis. I love you."

"I love you too. You take care now and I'll see ya on Thursday, ya hear? And… and uh don't forget those recipes."

"I won't. Bye."

"Bye.'

Mandi hung up the phone. The entire conversation was bittersweet. She was going to miss Francine, but saw it also as an opportunity to see Fletcher. Despite the fact she was happy with the husband she now had, something just told her to visit Fletcher. Though a tiny part of her still thought of him, she just wanted to know a bit more about him. However, she didn't know why. All she knew was that it was necessary. Though, she wouldn't dare tell Ronnie that she was going to go see him. All he was going to know was that she was attending Francine's funeral and would return Monday.

When Ronnie heard exactly that, he didn't mind. He wished Mandi the best, and promised to watch over the kids.

Wednesday of that week, Mandi returned to Mississippi. It was there she reunited with her father who was in town also to pay his last respects along with a few of her siblings.

The next day, on Thursday morning, she and her family went to the funeral. When they got there, there were a number of limos and expensive vehicles parked in front of the church. Many prominent people were present at the funeral, most of whom Mandi had never seen before. Yet it was clear that Francine was well recognized and respected by many people.

Walter Sullivan, Francine's brother, along with their sister, Annie, were also present. Josh, their other brother, had since died 12 years prior, while their mother, Mildred, died 10 years before Josh at age 78. Five of Francine's nine children, who were still living, showed up with their families to pay their final respects to their dear mother.

During the ceremony, a good number of people came to give their own personal testimonies about her, which was very emotional for Mandi. One particular guest who came to speak was Scarlet Allen, who was now Mrs. Williams. She was the young girl who Francine saved from an oncoming car back in Virginia 65 years earlier, which led Francine to meet Scarlet's mother, Mary Jo, who later became Francine's mentor.

Scarlet made some very moving remarks about Francine, telling how she and Mary Jo would communicate frequently while Scarlet listened in on their conversations. There was not one dry eye in that room.

Scarlet, who was now 68, was happily married with 6 children and 16 grandchildren. She now lived in Florida with her husband, Sherman, whom she had been married to for over 40 years. He was also at the funeral.

The main theme that Mandi heard people say repeatedly about Francine was that she had humility. Despite her wealth, she devoted her time and energy toward bettering humanity and helping others achieve their goals. About five people claimed how she aided in their growth and development, which helped them obtain the fortunes and happiness they had now. Some of them were couples who had their marriages restored after coming to Francine. It was very clear: Francine was truly a beloved woman and was going to be deeply missed. Nothing but sobs and cries filled the room.

It was at that moment Mandi understood exactly what Francine meant years ago when she said: *"It isn't what you have that's important. It's the person you become."* And through the numerous people who were present at that funeral, it was evident who Francine was. The impact she had on people's lives was in exact proportion to who she was as a person. People like her are never forgotten. They are immortalized. Why? Because it is the lives of the people they touched and left behind while on this earth that make it so; as true with Francine.

During this moment while sitting in one of the pews, Mandi unfolded a message from her pocket that Francine wrote to her long ago. It was a quote from Benjamin Disraeli to remind Mandi of what Francine tried to aspire to everyday. The message said:

"The greatest good you can do for another is not to share your riches, but reveal to him his own."

Mandi remembered Francine's hopes for her to reveal to someone else their own riches, just as Francine discovered hers through her rich mentor, Mary Jo.

When it was time for the burial, Mandi couldn't help but cling to her father, crying. People began dropping their roses on Francine's casket that was already placed six feet below the surface. Mandi tossed a red rose in the center before looking at the sky whispering, *Goodbye Francine, 'til we meet again.* She then walked away and hugged her father.

"You know what you have to do now," reminded Charlie, drying his eyes.

Mandi nodded.

"All right now. You made a promise. You have to keep to it. If not, you'll even let *me* down. You unduhstand? Francine deserves that."

Mandi nodded. "I will papa," she said. "I will."

"That's my girl. Okay, now let's go."

Soon after, the two of them strolled off with the rest of the family back to Charlie's house. Francine's tombstone later read something that couldn't have been closer to the truth. It read:

Francine
Ann
Williamson
A Teacher. A Savior.
A Warrior. A Friend.
1911-1991

As it turned out, even in death, Francine was never too far from her husband, John. Her grave ended up being placed right next to his, just as she had wanted. It was her final wish.

So long, Francine. So long. You were a beautiful inspiration to us all.

14

꧁꧂

Finding Fletch

The following day, Mandi prepared herself to go to the Skeegee County Jail to meet Fletcher. Carla was going to drive her there. Her appointment was at 1:30 p.m. Carla would wait in the car checking inventory reports for *Thelma's Secret* while her sister went in alone. When Mandi got there, she showed the guards her ID. She was then searched and entered through a couple gates, hopped on the elevator, and entered the hall to talk to Fletcher.

The room had a strange odor and looked dirty. It was composed of nine numbered glass windows where the visitors could see the prisoners and vice versa. And next to each window was a phone with which the inmates and visitors had to use to communicate.

After a few minutes, Fletcher came out in an orange prison outfit. He'd grown a heavy beard, and appeared more muscular than when Mandi had last seen him. A part of Mandi felt sorry for him. She could sense there was a sign of hopelessness and partial embarrassment when he saw that she was there. Yet a part of him felt real happy that Mandi had come to see him.

Mandi waved to him, and he waved back. He then went and sat at window #5, where Mandi picked up the phone. It was the closest they could get to each other.

"Hi," she said.

"Hi, Mandi. How're you doin'?"

"Fine."

"Man, it's been a long time. You still look good by the way. Much better than you did in high school."

"Thanks," she smiled. "How're you holding up in here?"

"Man," he said, shaking his head. "You don't ever want to be in here. This place has nothing you want. The value you have once you enter this cell goes way down dramatically. You're considered nothing. You mean nothing. You're worth nothing."

"Well, I'm sorry you feel that way."

"And I'm sorry too," he said.

"For what?"

"I'm deeply sorry for everything I did and how I hurt you. You didn't deserve any of that. You deserved better… "

"Fletch dear, the reason I came here was just to see you, all right? Not get a confession. I am over that now and have since moved on… *seriously*. I forgave you a long time ago and I realized now that it just wasn't meant to be. So don't worry about it. We were kids back then, remember?"

"That's right. We *were* kids. So tell me about yourself. What'ch ya doin' now?"

"Well first of all, I live in Detroit now. I'm happily married with three kids, ages 11, 8 and 6. Their names are Honey, Daisy and Riley. I graduated from Wayne University with a degree in psychology."

"Wow, that's good for you. Congratulations. I always knew you could do it. You were always the brightest in our class. Anyway... does yo' man treat you all right?"

"Yes he does, thank you very much. His name's Ronnie and he has his own construction company. Anything you have, he can fix it, guaranteed."

"Well that's good," Fletcher said, nodding his head. "I'm glad to see you're making progress."

"Thank you. Now listen Fletcher, we don't have a lot of time to talk. So let's talk about you. What happened?"

For a moment, Fletcher paused, thinking how to answer that question.

"You know Mandi, it's good we never got together. I've been a total mess. I've robbed and hurt people, used drugs, and even robbed a bank once. I have five felonies and am facing up to 10 years in prison for assault and attempted murder."

"You don't have to answer this if you don't want to, but... did you do these things they said you did to that woman?" Mandi asked.

Fletcher nodded. "The woman I attacked is in critical condition and when she gets out, she's gonna talk and blow the whistle. I already know that. All the prosecution is waiting on is for her to recover in case I want to push it to trial."

"Do you want to?"

Fletcher shook his head. "There's no need really," he said. "I admit I did it. My only concern is whether I can get a shorter sentence if I plead guilty."

Mandi looked down, shaking her head, before raising it again to glance at Fletcher.

"What made you act this way? Back in high school, you were never like this."

Fletcher shrugged his shoulders. "Just being with the wrong crowd, I guess. But you know what Mandi, there's a great number of people that don't belong in here and there's some others who are really not bad people but just made some mistakes and really don't know which way to go. Most of them grew up on bad advice and never got the proper guidance that would keep them from being here. I'm serious, if someone, maybe like you rather, could educate them on a better path like you have, maybe that might bring about change. As for me, I'm already going to prison, I know that. But if some of these guys that are getting out, could be shown a more positive light, then I don't think they'd ever come here anymore... since now they have something to live for."

Instantly Mandi's eyes lit up. She just couldn't believe what she was hearing. Was Fletcher suddenly an indirect messenger of the universe telling her what she needed to do to spread her mission? If so, preach on, Fletch. Preach on.

"Well... how... I mean how could I go about doing that... assuming *if* I chose to go that route?" inquired Mandi.

"Well for one, you could become a parole officer. Since the inmates would have to meet with you directly after they leave prison, you could be their personal counselor and teach them on ways they can improve their lives so they don't go back to jail. That's one way. Another way is to be a probation officer which is almost like a parole officer except that you're dealing with people that have less to lose, compared to people just coming out of prison who want to stay free. I mean the choice is up to you, but I feel being a parole officer is more effective."

Just then, one of the guards indicated that they had only 5 minutes left.

"Listen Fletcher, we don't have much time, but I want to thank you. Thank you. Thank you. Thank you. You've answered my prayers. That's what I'm going to do. I'm going to be a parole officer."

"Well all right. That's what I like to hear. But do you have any experience... "

"Doesn't matter," she said shaking her head." I'm going to be a parole officer and that's it. Period. End of story. I've made up my mind."

"Wow, that fast? Well… whatever it is, I'm glad I was able to help."

"I'm glad I was able to be here. And just so you know, no matter what ever happened, I still love you. That will never change. You were my first, remember? You don't ever forget your first."

Fletcher smiled. "That is true," he said. "Well, I've come to the conclusion that whatever will be, will be. It's my problem and I'm ready to take on whatever consequences."

"Well listen, you remember my sister, Carla?"

Fletcher nodded. "What about her?" he asked.

"I will see to it she follows your case in knowing where they're going to place you in case you're not here anymore. From there, I can write you from time to time to see how you're doing and let you know how things are with my endeavors as a parole officer."

"That's cool, but out of respect, Mandi, I just wanna say this. I still do care for you but you have a nice family; nice home. Don't mess it up because of me. I don't want you to be giving me any money for commissary or giving me phone cards to call you. What's done is in the past. So let's just leave it that way, okay? For your sake and mine."

"Okay."

"But still write me sometimes, though. Just don't do anymore than that. You've got a life. Okay? So do me a favor."

"What?"

"*Live* it."

Mandi smiled. "I will."

Just then, the guard indicated for the two of them to start wrapping it up.

"Well I have to get outta here now. But first, stretch out your left hand and place it against this glass here," he said.

Mandi did. Fletcher then did the same on his end, placing his right hand in position to match Mandi's left. "May God continue to keep you and your family safe and guide you in this journey you plan to embark upon. Amen."

"Amen," Mandi replied.

"Love ya and good luck," he said.

"Thanks, and stay strong, Okay?"

"Okay, peace."

They then hung up the phone together, removing their hands from the glass before Fletcher blew her a kiss, smiling. Mandi smiled as well and waved back to him until he was gone. It would be the last time they'd ever see each other.

In her mind, Mandi couldn't see how the same Fletcher who extended such words of love and inspiration could have ever committed such crimes. He seemed so intelligent. For a moment, she wondered if the police even had the right guy.

As she left the County building, Mandi was filled with so much joy and excitement. She had finally found her calling. While approaching the car where Carla waited, she couldn't help but smile emphatically.

"Uh oh, don't tell me," said Carla. "You're not in love with him again, are you?"

Mandi looked at her in smiles. "No, *better!* I'm going to be a parole officer. C'mon, let's go."

From there, they took off.

15

New
Journey

MANDI FELT BOTH EXHILARATED AND RENEWED AS SHE travelled back to Detroit. Upon finding Ronnie in the airport, she ran over to him, clinging to him hard. Ronnie, a bit surprised, just wrapped his arms around his wife, patting her gently on the back of the head.

"I will always remain grateful to God for giving me you. I love you so much and feel so honored and blessed to be your wife. Thank you *so* much for coming into my life," she said. "I love you."

Ronnie, who was surprised by the statement, didn't really know how to respond.

"Aw… are you all right?" he asked.

Mandi nodded her head. "I've never felt better," she replied.

Ronnie stood silent, thinking of something better to say. "I'm thankful for Him giving me you too," he said. "May you remain the person you are and never change. You always bring me such good luck and I'm a better man because of it. So I'm also very grateful; both to that... and the pineapple juice."

Mandi laughed before kissing him. "Francine was right all long," she whispered to herself.

"*What?*" wondered Ronnie.

Mandi appeared a bit startled, not knowing he was listening. "Oh uh... nothing," she said.

Ronnie glanced at her innocent smile. "So... what's the occasion?" he asked. "I mean why're you so excited?"

"I've just decided to become a parole officer."

"What?"

"A parole officer. I've made up my mind."

"Really?"

Mandi simply nodded.

Afterwards, the two of them walked away with Ronnie's arms wrapped around Mandi's shoulders.

"Say, why don't we do something special and lodge in a hotel for the night. My dad's with the kids now and I'm sure he won't mind."

"Well then why don't we just stay home together... rather than spending money?" Mandi asked.

"Remember... I want us to do something *special*," Ronnie answered after stopping to look at her.

Mandi was so excited to hear that. It showed all over her face. "Sure," she said. "Let's do it!"

"Great." Ronnie then kissed her forehead again. Due to the kids and his busy schedule, he rarely had time to spend with his wife alone. But he received a major contract from a large firm while Mandi was away, and wanted to take this opportunity to celebrate with her, especially since he figured none of that would have been possible without her. And he couldn't wait to tell her all about it.

"So... tell me more about this parole officer thing," he said. "Like what made you *really* decide to be one?"

Mandi just smiled at him and said, "It was the best fit I could come up with in carrying out my goals."

And in truth, she didn't lie.

By the time she finally got situated, Mandi began conducting research on the duties of a parole officer. What she found was quite similar to what Fletcher had told her. A parole officer, or PO as most would say, is in charge of supervising former inmates. They create a schedule for meeting with each offender based on the person's history and gravity of crime committed. During each meeting, there would be brief discussions, where the parole officer would interview the former inmate as to his or her welfare, and report any violation back to the assigning entity.

The parole officer would listen to the former inmates and possibly give some advice to help him or her. The parole officer initially had to indicate to the former inmate the extent of their parole and stress the rules that must be adhered to while on parole. Failure to comply could result in the client's return back to prison, which usually was decided by a judge. The parole officer was also required by law to administer drug screening at random to determine whether or not they were using illegal substances while out on the streets.

The great thing about this job, which Mandi found fascinating, was that since she would be dealing with adults, there wouldn't be any retaliation from family or friends as a result of any materials she would give out. For the most part, her clients would be hers, and rarely would any other staff have reason to question her style of work. All she needed was to make sure she completed the reports on all her clients in a timely fashion.

So in essence, Mandi saw this as the perfect fit for her. It didn't appear that it would be detrimental to teach her clients about the 'secret' if she chose to. Plus, since it was a government job, there were perks and benefits that came along with it. Also, it was her chance to see firsthand how law enforcement really worked.

So within a couple months, Mandi began the application process for a position in downtown Detroit.

Her excitement made the wait easy and ultimately led to the call. Three months later, she received a phone call and was hired to work on the 3rd floor of the Detroit Metro Parole Office, which was located a few buildings from the police headquarters. There, she had her own office with the basic equipment that came with it. She placed a picture of her family next to a large computer that sat on her desk. She kept a separate picture of her and Francine in the corner as a memory. Seeing that alone made Mandi proud.

During the coming months, Mandi would gradually get used to her new field. She would later learn through Carla that Fletcher was doing 7 years in prison for his crimes. While he was there, he converted to Islam, living humbly in his cell, reading his Quran. Such was the life he chose for himself both in prison and beyond. He sort of felt that prison was a good thing for him, due to the fact that it gave him the ability to reach out to other inmates who were as misguided as he was.

Some time would pass and Mandi was not able to find a consistent client willing to change their attitude and learn the techniques to living a better life. The exercise was a bit stressful to Mandi since most of the former inmates were so set in their old ways. Based on their attitudes, she already knew those same people would be back in prison very shortly. It was a culture already imbedded in them. It was only a matter of time. Yet whenever she stared at the picture of herself and Francine together, it gave her all the hope and encouragement she needed to move on to find that person who was willing to listen, learn and apply the methods.

A few more weeks would pass and it soon became early spring. It was 4 p.m. on a Friday afternoon, about a half hour before the parole division would close its operations for the day. Mandi, who was relieved, began roaming the hallways to use the time until it was 4:30 p.m.

She had a co-worker named Maria Gonzalez. Maria was a beautiful Puerto Rican with glasses, about the same age as Mandi, who also happened to be a good friend. They liked to chat and tell stories, which usually took place during break or near the end of the workday. Today was no different. Therefore, Mandi decided to visit and chat with her friend for a while.

Around this time, Mandi already knew Maria was not doing much of anything except for making her usual phone calls to family and friends. In fact, Maria always kept a principle that real work ended at 4 p.m. The other half hour was Uncle Sam's money, as far as she was concerned. So when Mandi stopped by, of course Maria was sitting at her desk reading *People* magazine in Spanish.

"Que paso?" Mandi greeted.

Maria looked up. "Hey, what's up?" she replied. She had a strong foreign accent that sounded kind of funny whenever she spoke fast.

"You ready for the weekend?" Mandi wondered.

"Si, who isn't? Anyone who isn't ready has to be one of three things. Either they're in jail, very sick, or have no pulse at all, which means they're either in the mortuary or graveyard. Da's it."

Mandi laughed. She and Maria shared the same humor, and Mandi enjoyed being with her. Afterwards, the two of them began having small talk until their supervisor, Mickey Giovanni, suddenly stepped into the office. He was a tall Italian guy, age 40.

"There you two are," he said. "Listen, I have a file that just came on my desk. The client's name is, Ja... Ja... I believe the name is pronounced Ja-Queee-ta... Jenkins. Yeah, that's it. JaQuita Jenkins. She also goes by the name Jackie. Anyway, according to the report, she's being released from prison after serving four years for assault to an officer and armed robbery. She's black, age 23 with no family to go to. Anyway, it's hot and ready. Who wants it?"

Both Maria and Mandi just looked at each other before turning to him without saying a word.

"Come on now," he said with enthusiasm. "Who wants it?"

"Not me," Maria said. "I have several files I still have to get done."

"Maria, when *don't* you have several files you still have to get done? You're the slowest worker I know. Sometimes I even wonder why you're still here," he joked.

"'Cause you never fire me."

Mickey had a tendency to always try to be funny, some of which was a bit overboard at times. However, he and Maria always joked around. Therefore, Maria never took offense. But they both knew their limits.

"Mandi, how 'bout you? You know you want it," he suggested.

"I have a bunch of files I have to get done, too."

The room remained silent for a moment. "C'mon ladies. I haven't got all day and I'm not paying you two overtime, either. So c'mon, who wants it?"

There was still no answer. "Okay then, we're going to play this lil' game called 'Eenee, meeni, mini, moe.' How's that?" suggested Mickey.

Still, no one answered. "Okay, here goes," he began, waving his finger around. "*Eenie meeni mini moe. Catch a...*"

"You don't have to do all that," uttered Mandi with annoyance. "Just make a decision, boss man."

Mickey looked at her strangely, pausing for a moment. "Okay. I will. Since *you* want to be so damn technical about it, *here*. It's yours," he said, handing it to Mandi. "I *was* going to give it to Maria anyway, since I know how the song ends. But since you opened your mouth, have fun."

Mandi took the file.

"I'm sure she will," remarked Maria happily.

Mandi gave her an awkward stare.

"All right, it's been fun ladies, but gotta run. You all have a good weekend now. Be safe... and... uh just so you know, we reopen back on Monday," said Mickey, before leaving. He always tried to be funny.

"Whatever," Mandi remarked softly, while shaking her head.

She then turned, glancing at Maria, who like a kid, stuck her tongue out at Mandi, teasing her.

Mandi just shrugged her shoulders, opening the file. "*So*," she remarked. "It doesn't bother me. Besides, you'll still have plenty more on your desk come Monday."

"Yeah, but guess what?"

"What?"

"Not *today*."

Mandi then made a fun gesture, trying to hand Maria the file, who instantly surrounded her desk, shaking her head. "No way, José," she laughed. "Not gonna happen. It's yours."

Mandi just smiled, amazed by Maria's expression. Mandi knew that Maria wouldn't take it. However, just seeing how she jumped up to protect her desk was hilarious in itself, and she wouldn't forget it.

"Relax. Trust me. It's not that serious," Mandi told her.

Mandi then turned around and began reading the file while still in Maria's office. Though, nothing major about the report really jumped out at her. But after dealing with tons of felony cases, all the stories seemed pretty much the same to her. After several minutes, Maria alerted Mandi that they had 15 minutes left before work was over. Mandi, who forgot all about the time while reading, began to head out of the office.

"Aw… you have a good weekend," she told Maria.

"You do the same," Maria replied. "Adios."

Mandi eventually went back to her office and sat down in her chair, dropping the file on her desk. She looked at the clock. It was now 4:18. So, in a hurry, she pulled out her desk drawer and grabbed some hand sanitizer to rub her hands. After, she opened up her computer to input the data from the file. Within minutes, it was official. The case was hers!

Soon after, she leaned against her chair, daydreaming while staring at her picture with Francine. For some strange reason while staring at it, Mandi got the funny feeling that Francine was suddenly looking straight back at her in the flesh, smiling, as if Mandi had just done something special of some sort. But after pondering that for a moment, Mandi suddenly heard the noise of workers rushing out, which signaled that it was finally time to go. She then shut off her computer, locked all the cabinets, turned off the lights, and grabbed her coat to take off as well.

From that moment on, unbeknownst to her, her magical journey as a mentor had just begun.

THE END

"A life is not important except in the impact it has on other lives."

—Jackie Robinson

Mandi's dreams came true. Now what would you like to manifest?

Start now by putting your name on the blank line and list all the things that you want in your life. Remember, no dream is too big or too small for the universe to deliver. After you're done, look at it every day for 10 minutes and read it aloud, believing that it will come in, and discover the magic that will appear into your life.

I, _____, would like to manifest the following in my life

Acknowledgments

I FIRST WANT TO GIVE FIRST AND FOREMOST THANKS AGAIN to Almighty God for His Infinite Power in blessing me as a writer. There is nothing that I can think of that can fully explain how I was able to develop the wisdom, strength, courage, and foresight in writing all my books. It is an aura that I can't explain nor fully comprehend for the life of me. All that I can say is that whatever this energy is, it definitely exists and is *real!* There is a power or Infinite Intelligence out there that is present always and available for any man who wishes to tap in to use it, which is what happened to me. And when it happened, all I did was follow suit, allowing spirit to lead me wherever it wanted me to go against all opposition and circumstances, and in effect, everything else took care of itself. I wish there was a better way I could explain how these books came to be, but this is the best conclusion I can come up with so far. And I'm okay with that. It was God, The Heavenly Father, that wrote this series and not me.

Next, I want to thank Uchechi, Ugochi, and Oluchi for being the girls that you are. Next, I want to thank my lovely parents for truly being there during my time of despair, adversity, and challenges. You truly do embody what love is truly all about. Through thick and thin, you have always been there for me and I am entirely indebted to you. My own goal is that I model that standard in my own life and those around me. Thank you.

Thanks Connie Gorofoli for your great professionalism! You truly are a wonderful editor. A different set of eyes always creates a newer perspective, which is what I experienced that helped make this classic what it is.

Thank you Russell for your unwavering talent and patience in making this all possible through the websites. I am always in awe with what you can do. I also appreciate you Nate for your cover design and layout. You've been there when I needed you.

To Beverly and Dr. Tracy Harris. You truly are friends for life. Thank you for your support and hanging in there with me. And thanks Amber Harris and Michelle "Mama Kimba" Posey for taking the time out for the cover.

I also want to commend Zora Neale Hurston for giving me that Southern style of writing through those rich stories of hers. You've been an inspiration and I learned a lot from the dialogues.

Thanks also for all you radio show hosts and endorsees of my book. You all truly are miracles. Despite all your busy schedules, thank you for taking time out to review my work. You'll never be forgotten. Last but not least, I want to thank the whole L.I.F.E. Leadership Group for your life changing information that has definitely impacted my life a great deal. The same for the whole WIN group and all its members. I love you guys!

As for anyone else, thanks so much for your love and support. Keep smiling and don't ever let anyone steal your dream!

Peace and love.

Experience the Miracle Trilogy® Classic Series

AVAILABLE NOW!

Mandi's mentor

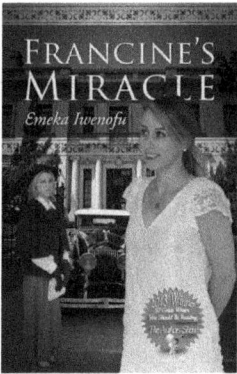

"Francine's Miracle *is delightful. Once again, Emeka Iwenofu creates a character that readers relate to; first in her struggles and then in her ultimate triumph. The story of Francine's journey is a powerful tribute to the miracles that happen when one woman learns to harness the power within to manifest the life of her dreams. If you want to be inspired, read this book!*"
—Lisa Ryan, Chief Appreciation Strategist, *Grategy*
Author of *The Upside of Down Times: Discoveringthe Power of Gratitude*
Featured expert in "The Keeper of the Keys" and
"The Gratitude Experiment"

FrancinesMiracle.com

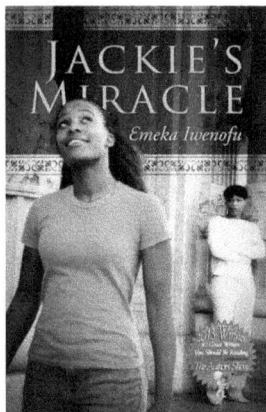

Sources

Allen, James. *As a Man Thinketh*. Jeremy P. Tarcher/Penguin. New York, NY. 1902

Bristol, Claude M. *The Magic of Believing*. Pocket Books. New York, NY. 1948

Byrne, Rhonda. *The Secret*. Atria Books; New York, NY. Beyond Words Publishing; Hillsboro, OR. 2006

Carnegie, Dale. *How to Win Friends and Influence People*. Simon & Schuster. New York, NY. 1936

Conwell, Russell H. *Acres of Diamonds*. Jeremy P. Tarcher/Penguin. New York, NY. 1915

Dherbier, Yann-Brice / Verlhac, Pierre-Henri. *John Fitzgerald Kennedy: A Life in Pictures*. Phaisdon Press. New York, NY. 2003

Giblin, Les. *How to Have Power and Confidence in Dealing with People*. Reward Books. New York, NY. 1956

Hill, Napoleon. *The Law of Success in Sixteen Lessons*. Tribeca Books. New York, NY. 1928

Hill, Napoleon / Stone, W. Clement. *Success Through a Positive Mental Attitude*. Pocket Books. New York, NY. 1960

Hill, Napoleon. *Think and Grow Rich*. Jeremy P. Tarcher/Penguin. New York, NY. 1937

Maltz, Maxwell. *Psycho-cybernetics*. Pocket Books. New York, NY. 1960

Mandino, Og. *The Greatest Salesman in the World*. Bantum Books. New York, NY. 1968

Martin, Francis P. *Hung by the Tongue*. FPM Publications. Lafayette, LA. 1979

Peale, Norman Vincent. *The Power of Positive Thinking*. Fireside. New York, NY. 1952

Schwartz, David. J. *The Magic of Thinking Big*. Simon & Schuster. New York, NY. 1959

Wattles, Wallace D. *The Science of Getting Rich*. Jeremy P. Tarcher/Penguin. New York, NY. 1910

Ziglar, Zig. *See You at the Top*. Pelican Publishing Company, Inc. Gretna, LA. 1975

Success Audio. Speaker: John Maxwell. CD Audio. Video-Plus. Dallas, TX. 2009

The Global Information Network. *Your Wish is Your Command*. Speaker: Kevin Trudeau. CD Audio Set. 2009

Eyes on the Prize: America's Civil Rights Years 1954-1964. PBS Home Video. Blackside. Alexandria, VA. 1987

Faces in the Water: The Martyrs of the Civil Rights Memorial. Southern Poverty Law Center Production. Montgomery, AL. 2005

Forks Over Knives. Monica Beach Media. Los Angeles, CA. 2011

Freedom Song. TNT Original. Turner Films, Inc. Atlanta, GA. 2000

Idlewild. HBO Films. Mosaic Media Group. Universal Studios. Universal City, CA. 2006

Ray. Bristol Bay Productions. Universal Studios. Universal City, CA. 2004

The Kennedys. Muse Entertainment. Asylum Entertainment. Montreal, Canada. 2011

Waiting for Superman. Participant Films. Paramount Pictures. Hollywood, CA. 2010

"The Closer I Get to You". Artists: Roberta Flack, Donny Hathaway. Atlantic Records. 1978.

http://en.wikipedia.org/wiki/Emmett_Till

http://en.wikipedia.org/wiki/James_Meredith

http://en.wikipedia.org/wiki/John_f._kennedy#Civil_rights

http://en.wikipedia.org/wiki/Medgar_Evers

http://en.wikipedia.org/wiki/Muddy_Waters

http://en.wikipedia.org/wiki/Patton

http://en.wikipedia.org/wiki/Ray_charles

http://en.wikipedia.org/wiki/The_Temptations

http://globalinformationnetwork.com/Members/The-Se-crets/Member-1-Secrets.aspx
Audio: Patton on Leadership (part 3 of 4)

http://www.splcenter.org/civil-rights-memorial/civil-rights-martyrs

http://www.youtube.com/watch?v=JgUc7eLXsOs
Keyword: The Strangest Secret in the World

http://www.youtube.com/watch?v=ajIRxdeCRZM
Keyword: The Strangest Secret (part 1 of 3)

http://www.youtube.com/watch?v=es7UjzlSRcU
Keyword: The Strangest Secret (part 2 of 3)

http://www.youtube.com/watch?v=AuPdzHd8idk&feature=
related
Keyword: The Strangest Secret (part 3 of 3)

https://www.youtube.com/watch?v=k3Ya5qiiW6k
Keyword: Zeitgeist: The Movie (2007)

About the Author

EMEKA IS A YOUNG ASPIRING author who attained a degree in accounting before encountering challenges in life that led him to pursue his passion for writing while going on a personal mission to help inspire people on how to live abundantly and happily through the techniques he discusses in his series The Miracle Trilogy® which has been adored and admired by fans throughout the world, from which *Jackie's Miracle* has been translated into Japanese with more translations of all three of his books, expected in the near future.

Since publishing *Jackie's Miracle*, Emeka has been busy appearing on multiple radio stations as well as doing weekly blogs on his websites, sharing his mission to the world of positive thought and spirituality and the keys to successful living which he models daily in his life.

He is the owner of Hope Point Press and is the winner of the coveted *2013 Fifty Great Writers You Should Be Reading Award* from The Author Show as well as the 2014 Award for *Mandi's Miracle*. He hopes his books continue to inspire people of all walks of life into realizing that they themselves control their destiny and can create a more fulfilling, prosperous, and rewarding life for themselves if they really want to.

www.ingramcontent.com/pod-product-compliance
Lightning Source LLC
Chambersburg PA
CBHW072002040426
42447CB00009B/1442